Cambridge Elements

Elements in Musical Theatre
edited by
William A. Everett
University of Missouri-Kansas City

GYPSY AND THE BROADWAY MUSICAL MADWOMAN

A Feminist Analysis

Mary Beth Sheehy
Independent Scholar

CAMBRIDGE
UNIVERSITY PRESS

Shaftesbury Road, Cambridge CB2 8EA, United Kingdom

One Liberty Plaza, 20th Floor, New York, NY 10006, USA

477 Williamstown Road, Port Melbourne, VIC 3207, Australia

314–321, 3rd Floor, Plot 3, Splendor Forum, Jasola District Centre,
New Delhi – 110025, India

103 Penang Road, #05-06/07, Visioncrest Commercial, Singapore 238467

Cambridge University Press is part of Cambridge University Press & Assessment,
a department of the University of Cambridge.

We share the University's mission to contribute to society through the pursuit of
education, learning and research at the highest international levels of excellence.

www.cambridge.org
Information on this title: www.cambridge.org/9781009552264

DOI: 10.1017/9781009552271

First published 2025

A catalogue record for this publication is available from the British Library

ISBN 978-1-009-55226-4 Hardback
ISBN 978-1-009-55231-8 Paperback
ISSN 2631-6528 (online)
ISSN 2631-651X (print)

Cambridge University Press & Assessment has no responsibility for the persistence
or accuracy of URLs for external or third-party internet websites referred to in this
publication and does not guarantee that any content on such websites is, or will remain,
accurate or appropriate.

For EU product safety concerns, contact us at Calle de José Abascal, 56, 1°, 28003
Madrid, Spain, or email eugpsr@cambridge.org

Gypsy and the Broadway Musical Madwoman

A Feminist Analysis

Elements in Musical Theatre

DOI: 10.1017/9781009552271
First published online: May 2025

Mary Beth Sheehy
Independent Scholar

Author for correspondence: Mary Beth Sheehy, sheehy.marybeth@gmail.com

Abstract: *Gypsy*, the groundbreaking 1959 Broadway musical by Jule Styne, Stephen Sondheim, and Arthur Laurents, introduced the world of musical theater to one of the most formidable female characters ever to strut onto the stage: Madam (Momma) Rose. She embodies the archetypal "stage mother" whose lifelong journey to achieve fame, enacted vicariously through her daughters and their vagabond life across America, drives her to a "madness" akin to that of the quintessential operatic madwoman. Her famous mad scene, "Rose's Turn," demonstrates the many analytical possibilities intrinsic to this character definition.

The creators of *Gypsy*'s Rose thus showcased the "Broadway musical madwoman" type: a female character who, like her foremother the operatic madwoman, is rife with gendered complexity that creates a fascinating opportunity for feminist analytical study. This Element's two-pronged approach uses the frameworks of feminist theory and musicological analysis to consider the importance, legacy, and reception of Rose's journey.

Keywords: musical theater, *Gypsy*, Broadway, feminist, madwoman

ISBNs: 9781009552264 (HB), 9781009552318 (PB), 9781009552271 (OC)
ISSNs: 2631-6528 (online), 2631-651X (print)

Contents

1 Overview of *Gypsy* and the Broadway Musical Madwoman

Introduction

Gypsy: a complex musical with an operatic "madwoman" at its helm. That is a workable, nutshell description of *Gypsy: A Musical Fable*, the 1959 Broadway show that turned the genre on its head. *Gypsy*'s protagonist, Rose, a complicated mother and a delusional fame-seeker, has become an emblematic character on Broadway who represents many feminist ideals while also embodying the problematic romanticism of the madwoman and fall to her demise with a glorious mad scene, "Rose's Turn." Operatic in its dramatic depth yet robed in the vestiges of the contemporary Broadway musical, *Gypsy* ushered in a new era of American musical theater, blending the thematic elements of opera, vaudeville, and the musical play. A somewhat twisted rendition of the archetypal American dream tale, it tells the life story of famous burlesque performer Gypsy Rose Lee through the exploits of the eponymous character's mother, Rose Hovick, from her daughter's childhood in vaudeville through her rise to striptease fame.

The analyses in this Element demonstrate how Rose progressively descends into "madness" throughout the course of *Gypsy*'s plot and score, exploring how the musical adaptation creates a madwoman in many places where she did not exist in the original source, Gypsy Rose Lee's memoir. The question of *why* the creators of *Gypsy* turned Rose into a madwoman is ultimately answered in my comparison of the musical to opera: elevation of the genre. Aleksei Grinenko's book *Seriously Mad: Mental Distress and the Broadway Musical* presents the notion that "from the midcentury on, the stage musical has exploited the symbolic capital of psychoanalytic views of interiority to shore up its aspirations to the domain of 'serious' art theater" (Grinenko, 2023: 2). Grinenko argues that, in *Gypsy*, "madness, endowed with a preeminent power to articulate and transmit insights and sway the audience, comes to stand for theater par excellence" (Grinenko, 2023: 11). My analytical goal, then, in comparing Rose to an operatic madwoman, and "Rose's Turn" to an operatic mad scene, is to substantiate this notion of "serious theater," as well as explore the spectator's viewpoint of Rose's madness from a feminist perspective.

Within the broader framework of the topic of the "madwoman," *Gypsy*'s Rose is important both in the Broadway musical's history and historiography. Historically speaking, *Gypsy* was written at the start of a turning point in musical theater, representing a category that straddled the "Golden Age" style of contemporary works by writers such as Rodgers and Hammerstein and the highly serious, more conceptual style of Stephen Sondheim, who served as *Gypsy*'s lyricist. Although preceded on the Broadway stage by maddened female protagonists such as Wanda in *Rose-Marie* (1924) and Azuri in *The Desert Song* (1926), *Gypsy*'s Rose stands apart for its musical legacy and stage legacy, having been revived on Broadway five times (1974, 1989, 2003, 2008, and 2024), once in the West End (2015) after its 1973 premiere, and two film versions (1962 and 1993). Holding such a crucial place in the Broadway canon and in musical theater history, Rose could be considered the "mother" of the contemporary Broadway musical madwoman – creating a long legacy of madwoman protagonists in hit Broadway productions that followed in the decades after *Gypsy* – and thus invites a great deal of analytical attention.[1] This Element's contribution to the show's historiography includes a detailed comparison of the musical's libretto to the original source, examination of journalistic reviews, and musical analysis of multiple numbers, including Rose's "mad scene."

Labeled a "musical fable" possibly because its plot seems more like a fairy-tale than real life, *Gypsy* is hard to categorize within the musical theater canon. It possesses heavy themes like many of Rodgers and Hammerstein's hits such as *South Pacific*, which addresses the topics of racism and war, or *Carousel*, which tackles difficult concepts such as domestic abuse – but *Gypsy* possesses none of the love-story themes featured in these shows. Nor is it an operatic dark tale like later Sondheim musicals, such as *Sweeney Todd*. It is not the typical brash Ethel Merman comedy of earlier decades, such as *Annie Get Your Gun*. *Gypsy* also does not fit emphatically into the Golden Age musical style category, not only because it blends musical comedy with serious thematic content as well as vaudeville-inspired numbers, but also because it excludes many key elements of that formulaic mid-century style. Sondheim explains how he and Styne wrote *Gypsy* "in the Rodgers and Hammerstein musical form – where you take a story and tell it with scene-song-scene-song, where peaks of emotion are carried forward into song" (Sondheim, in Gordon, 1992: 99). However, *Gypsy* also positions itself outside of that form in numerous ways. There is no true chorus, no title song, and neither is there a true romantic plot line or a likeable hero. As critic Walter Kerr wrote after seeing *Gypsy*'s opening night on Broadway: "I'm not sure whether 'Gypsy' is new fashioned, or old-fashioned, or integrated, or non-integrated. The only thing I'm sure of is that it's the best damn musical I've seen in years" (Kerr, 1959).

In this vein, and taking it a step further by comparing *Gypsy* to the fully integrated and emotion-packed genre of opera, *Gypsy* in many ways embodies what musicologist Richard Taruskin calls "tragicomedy," the category embraced

---

[1] These shows include, among others: *Chicago* (1975), *Sweeney Todd* (1979), *Sunset Boulevard* (1994), and *Next to Normal* (2009).

by nineteenth-century Italian opera composer Giuseppe Verdi. Quoting Verdi's contemporary Alessandro Manzoni, Taruskin describes this genre particularly in the context of adaptations of Shakespeare, a "mixture of the grave and the burlesque, the touching and the low" (Taruskin 2010: 576). While *Gypsy* is not exactly adapted from the likes of Shakespeare, the definition holds true. *Gypsy* is simultaneously funny and serious, light and dark, low-brow and high-brow. Thus, as a Broadway musical-style "tragicomedy," *Gypsy* the musical takes the story of Gypsy Rose Lee's memoir from a fabulous autobiographical tale into the "fable" that Larry Stempel describes as "[defying] the stereotype: a musical comedy with a meaning; a musical comedy with a mad scene" (Stempel, 2010: 454).

In defining Rose as a madwoman of operatic proportions, I borrow from Susan McClary's notion of *excess*, that female madness is "delineated musically through repetitive, ornamental, or chromatic excess" and that "normative [musical] procedures representing reason are erected around them to serve as protective frames" for other non-mad characters (McClary, 1991: loc. 1236). This analytical approach as applied to *Gypsy* incorporates detailed interpretation of the musical style, lyrical framing, virtuoso singing methods, and motivic repetition that appear in Rose's musical numbers throughout *Gypsy*, most especially in "Rose's Turn." In terms of framing Rose's excess, I consider the "sane lenses" through which the audience is guided to view Rose as mad; namely, the lens of Herbie, who I call the "male moral compass," and the lens of her two daughters, June and Louise (later known as Gypsy Rose Lee). These frames appear in both libretto and score. In Section 2, I consider the creation of the Herbie frame in the musical adaptation from the original source book. In Sections 3 and 4, I examine the frames as set within Rose's musical numbers.

I also define Rose's madness as being signified by her clear departures from "reality" throughout *Gypsy*'s plot and score. Rose's frequent delusions, her "dreams," are present in the libretto; musically, they are witnessed particularly in the use of motivic repetition. As Joseph Straus explains, a frequent manifestation of madness in musical contexts is the hearing of voices, often represented musically through repeated quotations (Straus, 2018: 94).

The most glaring representation of Rose's madness in *Gypsy* is, of course, in the mad scene: Rose's final number, "Rose's Turn." My analysis of *Gypsy*'s "mad scene" in Section 4 is two-pronged, considering both the music and the performance. Regarding the latter, I examine interpretation of the role by three Broadway and West End performers: Ethel Merman, Angela Lansbury, and Imelda Staunton, analyzing the concept of agency around Rose's descent into "madness" during this scene. For although the musical's creators wrote "Rose's Turn" as an operatic mad scene, the performers themselves possess the agency to interpret that mad scene in their own fashions. This dynamic creates a "feminist gaze" – but also one rife with the complexities of acting "madness" as a mental state.

In this Element's exploration of Rose as an operatic madwoman, the underlying question remains: can Rose's madness be subversive, or feminist, especially considering the problematic nature of operatic madwomen and their demises under the patriarchy? The answer is complicated. There is a difference between representation and exploitation of "madness" as a character trait; the former engenders acceptance, the latter stigmatization. Too often the real representations of mental illness take a back seat to the spectacular elements of horror, satire, or melodrama. Furthermore, when madness is embodied specifically by a mad*woman*, the issues of representation are further complicated by the feminist concerns of gender and power dynamics. Whether she is oversexualized, violent, obsessive, or delusional, the madwoman exists within a gendered framework.

Analysis of madwomen on the musical stage continuously raises the question of agency: do they gain control through their madness, or does their madness control them? Catherine Clément argues that the operatic madwoman's madness liberates her and represents ultimate happiness; madness is an escape from the patriarchal controls that have determined the madwoman's life until the point of her mad scene. Using Donizetti's titular character from *Lucia di Lammermoor* as an exemplar of the trope, she explains,

> [Lucia] dismisses those who are separated from her forever, those who do not comprehend how perfectly complete is her joy. The curtain falls on Lucia's jubilation, set free and rising still . . . she is a "demented woman," but she is happy. (Clément, 1988: 89–90)

Other scholars disagree, however, with the notion that a woman's madness leads to her liberation or incites feminist sympathy. Elaine Showalter argues that even murderous madwomen do not escape male domination. Rather, they escape "one specific, intolerable exercise of women's wrongs by assuming an idealized, poetic form of pure femininity as the male culture had construed it: absolutely irrational, absolutely emotional, and, once the single act is accomplished, absolutely passive" (Showalter, 1985: 17). While both scholarly interpretations of the madwoman reveal the male-dominated frame in which she operates, their analytical conclusions are diametrically opposed: Clément considers her a hero, while Showalter believes her to be a victim.

Susan McClary provides a more nuanced view of the madwoman in this regard. She agrees with Clément's assessment, but her analysis of Lucia's madness-inspired freedom relates to the musical characterization; she argues that "Lucia has far too much energy" for the narrow confines" of typical musical structures. Thus, she explains, we should not "read Lucia solely as an instance of feminine dementia … For in her revolt against patriarchal oppression and musical conformity, she is also a romantic hero whose energy defies stifling social convention" and her music makes her powerful. "Her tragic end potentially enflames the resentment of all kinds … and, because she is mad, Lucia cannot, of course, be held responsible for deliberate resistance. Thus she can be victim and heroine simultaneously – in short, a martyr" (McClary, 1991: loc. 1402).

McClary's both/and approach frames the madwoman with the complexity required of this multidimensional trope. Ultimately, Lucia is both hero and victim; she kills Arturo and she is musically resonant, yet she must be mad – outside the frame of the norm – in order to accomplish her victory, and consequently dies. The madwoman's mad scene exposes the patriarchy, even if she cannot survive this act; thus, although the operatic madwoman is confined by her madness, she is simultaneously empowered by it. Borrowing this theoretical stance, I analyze *Gypsy*'s Rose an anti-hero in her own plot trajectory, her madness rendering her both victorious and defeated, each in their own complicated fashion.

Mary Ann Smart, however, states that while "madness is one of the few ways an operatic heroine can escape the near-inevitable plot process of seduction and death," such an interpretation "may too easily lead to the conclusion that all structures are male and repressive, and all freedom is female and positive: a difficult position in any creative context, since most works of art depend on structure in order to communicate" (Smart, 1992: 119–120).

Carolyn Abbate further complicates madwomen's positionality within an operatic performance; she posits that in operas featuring women, the female voice makes the performer an authorial figure because hearing a female voice is a "complicated phenomenon" in which "visually, the character singing is the passive object of our gaze. But aurally, she is resonant; her musical speech drowns out everything in range, and we sit as passive objects, battered by that voice" (Abbate, 1993: 254). Abbate demonstrates how a female opera lead possesses this voice and thus renders a power otherwise unavailable to her within the male authorship of the opera. Abbate's theoretical stance proves particularly useful for the analysis of *Gypsy* because she discusses music written by men for female characters and actors; *Gypsy*'s entire primary writing and productive team, with the exception of the female lead performers, was male. Thus, to calculate the creative power of women in musicals, the analyses in this Element consider the authorial voice as theorized by Abbate. The voice of the belting diva of musical theater can be interpreted in much the same way as the virtuoso voice of the operatic prima donna – for example, the brash and loud belt-style singing by Rose in *Gypsy* as established by the character's originator, Ethel Merman.

However, even when a female performer creates, exaggerates, or reclaims a character's madness, problems remain inherent to the madwoman trope. Megan Jenkins, for example, steers away from Abbate's notion of authorial voice in favor of a more disability-centered approach. Jenkins argues that "madness is a social construct that is often used to control individuals' behavior, especially women's" and so she aims to be "part of the movement of humanist scholars who seek to challenge sexist and heterosexist deployment of mental illness diagnoses" (Jenkins, 2010: 1–2). Within operatic frameworks, Jenkins posits, madness is most often a punishment for transgression against gender or sexual norms, and this correlation complicates an audience's understanding and stigmatization of mental illness.

Madness and Women in the Early and Mid Twentieth Century: Contextualizing Rose

Megan Jenkins explains that

> While opera and opera reception are valuable resources for scholars to examine the culture, politics, and history that gave rise to that specific work, it is important to remember that we are examining representations of madness, and not actual physical or psychical experiences of madness ... These characters – even when based on real people's lives – are crafted to represent contemporaneous conceptions of madness. (Jenkins, 2010: 9–10)

The "contemporaneous conception of madness" at the time of *Gypsy*'s creation aligns with American society in the early and mid twentieth century. Rose's plot trajectory is an extreme version of the quintessential "American dream" that permeates American culture.

Rose's pursuit of a fabled American romanticism in her chosen enterprise, show business, is relatable, not only to the mid-century audience of *Gypsy*'s original Broadway run, who lived in close historical proximity to the 1920s and 1930s era in which *Gypsy* is set, but to the perennial American audience as well. The "rags to riches" success story pervades both the Broadway musical canon – as shown in *My Fair Lady* (1956), *Funny Girl* (1964), and *Annie* (1977), just to name a few – and the larger American Zeitgeist. In an interview for *The New York Times*, Sondheim says that "the fact that [Rose is] monstrous to her daughters and the world is secondary ... She's a very American character, a gallant figure and a life force" (Rich, 2003).

However "secondary," Rose's relationship to her daughters – and her very identity as a mother – is a key component of her character, and her positioning within the patriarchal culture she fights so hard against. Keith Garebian explains in *The Making of* Gypsy that Rose is

> a larger-than-life representation of American Mom-ism, that syndrome that so bedevils many a generation that feel smothered by the hand that rocks the cradle and tightens the silver cord … When her turn comes to dream for herself, she seizes it with the sort of rough readiness that we, not inappropriately, identify as the essence of American enterprise and opportunism. (Garebian, 1994: 12)

According to Garebian's statement, those two aspects – Rose's "Mom-ism" and her opportunism – are deeply connected, although they both drive her in different ways. Rose's opportunism depends on her motherhood (because her enterprise is her daughters, themselves), but ultimately, she resents the fact that her motherhood gets in the way of her own success – as she portrays in "Rose's Turn."

Rose's most "grievous" sin in *Gypsy*, some would argue, is when she does finally achieve success, but at the cost of her daughter's "morals," in the moment she pushes teenage Louise into the world of burlesque. Of course, Rose's sense of "morals" has never truly existed; Herbie's character serves as a sort of moral compass for Rose's actions – as discussed in Section 2 – but for Rose, burlesque is simply the last exit on her show business odyssey. Ethan Mordden argues, "That Rose sends Louise out into the sleazy darkness of burlesque to strip, losing her lover [Herbie] but creating a star, tells us what Rose is: an American. Nothing matters but making it, stardom" (Mordden, 1998: 248). Similarly, Howard Kissel explains that "Rose's hunger for success through her daughters is so desperate, so unyielding that she forces Louise into burlesque, a huge and humiliating step down from vaudeville" (Kissel, in Engel, 2006: 23).

Some viewers may interpret Rose's hand in Louise's career shift into "sleazy" burlesque as the action of a madwoman, deranged by her greed for success. This interpretation adheres to the notion that the cultural Zeitgeist of 1959 America would not accept a "positive" representation of mother figure who sends her daughter into an "immoral" life as a stripper; thus, Rose was instead written as a complicated, monstrous, or even unhinged mother figure for her role in kick-starting Gypsy Rose Lee's career. However, a more nuanced point of view is also possible. On the one hand, Rose is portrayed as mad during the scene in which she pushes Louise onto the burlesque stage. In a manic monologue, Rose exclaims to Louise,

> Baby, it's all right to walk out when they want you. But you can't walk out
> now when after all these rotten years, we're still a flop . . . Just do this, so we
> can walk away proud because we made it! Maybe only in burlesque, maybe
> only in second rate burlesque at that – but let's walk away a star! (Laurents,
> 1959: 2–4–34)[2]

On the other hand, however, there is irony in Rose's ramblings – because Louise really does make it; the audience knows that Gypsy Rose Lee becomes a huge success not just as a stripper, but as an author, comedian, talk show host, and of course, the real-life inspiration behind this very Broadway musical. As shown in her Act II strip sequence, Louise subverts the definition of "stripping" by demonstrating the innovations that became the hallmark of Gypsy Rose Lee's career: not emphasizing the removal of clothing, but rather focusing on the "tease" in striptease by adding humor, commentary, and personal flair to her routines. Through these innovations, Gypsy Rose Lee gains agency and creates a "feminist gaze," much like that of Rose in her striptease sequence of "Rose's Turn," as discussed in Section 4.

Maya Cantu explores both Louise's and Rose's subversion of the American dream – in Louise's success as a stripper, and in Rose's choice to live life on the road and relentlessly pursue her dreams despite the difficulties that arise from being a woman and a mother on such a journey. Cantu explains how Rose defies the story's two main male characters, Pop and Herbie, who encourage her to settle down. She argues that *Gypsy*, along with other musicals in the 1950s such as *Happy Hunting* (1956) and *Once Upon a Mattress* (1959), "powerfully adapted the most transformative of fairy tale icons to address changes for American women both in the labor force and in the public sphere," which ultimately "meaningfully contributed to women's liberation" in the mid twentieth century (Cantu, 2015: 201). Similarly, in a review of *Gypsy* for *The Baltimore Sun*, Margaret McManus claimed Rose as "a symbol of independence and strength. She's loud and gusty and free-wheeling. She is the master of her fate" (McManus, 1959).

Not only does Rose embody a complicated version of motherhood, she also lives a lifestyle that subverts the domestic expectations of mothers in the early and mid twentieth century. Throughout Rose's show business odyssey in *Gypsy*, she is placed at an impossible crossroads: is she a "bad" mother for wanting something more for her daughters – and simultaneously herself? Or should she

---

[2] Throughout this document, I analyze stage directions and lines as quoted in two different versions
of the script. The first is the original 1959 script; the second, which I primarily use, is the widely
published Theater Communications Group edition, published in 1989. The two versions show
slight differences, but nothing that drastically changes any particular scene or character. I use both
in order to create a fuller picture of the scenes and broader analysis of the characters.

instead listen to the advice of the men in her life and settle down and live a domestic, "normal" life?

In their introduction to the edited book *"Bad" Mothers*, Molly Ladd-Taylor and Lauri Umansky list "the pushy stage mother" as one of the "bad" mothers who "moved noticeably toward center stage in American culture" in the second half of the twentieth century, noting that "women classed as 'bad' mothers" often include "those who did not live in a 'traditional' nuclear family" (Ladd-Taylor and Umanksy, 1998: 2–3). Rose fits their description of an unjustly labeled "bad" mother, her nontraditional parenting methods making her an Other. She constantly swims against the current of American culture by following her own ideals of "good" motherhood, regardless of the pushback she receives from her father and from Herbie, her own daughters (especially June), and, on a meta level, the audience itself. One of Rose's most indicative lines in the show is a response to Herbie, who claims that "[Louise] and June should both be in school," to which Rose quickly retorts: "And be just like other girls; cook and clean and sit and die!" (Laurents, 1989: 34).

Some of Rose's actions that appear "bad" or even "mad" – like prohibiting her daughters from attending school – are, in fact, fueled in part by a desire to escape heteronormative domesticity and gendered expectations of women. A statement from the real Rose Hovick to her daughters supports this assertion; in a letter dated November 2, 1944, she complained about their claim that they never went to school. She wrote,

> Some day [*sic*] the public will know the truth about your mother and they I am sure will not condemn me like you girls have done. I have a clear conscience thank God for the way I raised you both and I how I did all I could for you with what I had to do with. (Quinn, 2013: xii)

Richard Oakman examines *Gypsy* as one of the most important musical shows to portray the "mother archetype," alongside shows such as *Dreamgirls*, *Miss Saigon*, and *South Pacific*. Quoting Simone de Beauvoir's influential feminist text *The Second Sex*, he argues that "Rose is void of the 'defects of femininity' and she is able to retain an element of her autonomy" by resisting the patriarchal encouragement of her father – and, thereby, the patriarchal boundaries of domesticity norms in American culture (Oakman, 2017: 57).

Maya Cantu similarly argues that "the character of Rose represented a powerful repudiation of the 1950s Cinderella mythology, and an implicit subversion of the feminine mystique" (Cantu, 2015: 196). This "feminine mystique" references the concepts outlined in Betty Friedan's book *The Feminine Mystique*, published in 1963, just four years after *Gypsy*'s premiere. In this book, Friedan outlines the sexist problems inherent to female domesticity in mid twentieth-century American culture. The common "housewife" occupation, Friedan notes, leads to women facing a serious lack of identity, purpose, and independence from men. Although criticized for its focus on middle- and upper-class white women, Friedan's work was also lauded for sparking multiple feminist movements in the years following its publication. In many ways, *Gypsy*'s Rose represents the second-wave feminist woman – the "solution" to the housewife problem – outlined in *The Feminine Mystique*. If one thing is clear about Rose throughout *Gypsy*, it is that she does have a life's purpose; she refuses to adhere to the gendered domestic standards inherent in marriage and a "settled down" life.

Jennifer Worth agrees with this notion, stating that in *Gypsy*, "Momma Rose's household is a mockery of domesticity" (Worth, 2016: 257). She also posits, however, that the mother–daughter bond is portrayed as "pathologized, characterized by competition and aggression as much as by love and nurturance" (Worth, 2016: 259). She ultimately argues that Rose's life choices allow her independence, but at the cost of her daughters' happiness; later analysis of the number "If Momma was Married" in Section 3 considers this possibility.

Rose's lifestyle and motherhood, fueling the madness that finally rears its head in "Rose's Turn," can thus be interpreted in multiple ways. Rose's actions within the patriarchal structure of mid twentieth-century American society render her complex within a feminist analytical structure.

2 *Gypsy*'s Creative History: Inventing Rose

Gypsy's creators included composer Jule Styne (1905–1994), lyricist Stephen Sondheim (1930–2021), book writer Arthur Laurents (1917–2011), director/ choreographer Jerome Robbins (1918–1998), and producers David Merrick (1911–2000) and Leland Hayward (1902–1971). From the onset, actress Ethel Merman (1908–1984), who played Rose, was also involved in the creative process. Merrick originally bought the rights to Gypsy Rose Lee's (1911– 1970) published memoir. Although Gypsy Rose Lee labeled the work an autobiography, she admitted to fabricating many details of the memoir for the sake of entertainment. Her son Erik emphasizes this notion, explaining in the Afterword of a later edition of the memoir that "historical accuracy was much less important to her than a good punch line. She was, after all, an entertainer first and a writer second" (Lee, 1999: 346).

Arthur Laurents notes a similar realization about Gypsy's memoir being a fictionalized account. He explains that when he interviewed her while writing the musical's book, "her answer to any question was always amusing but no answer explained anything . . . " and she finally purportedly said to him, "Oh, darling, I've given so many versions, why don't you make up your own?" (Laurents, 2000: 379). Thus, the Rose of both the memoir and the musical is more a fictional character rather than a historical person, made larger-than-life in each of her transitions from reality to memoir to stage.

Gypsy's creative history began in 1958, just a year after the publication of the memoir. Arthur Laurents was, according to his own account, taken by the character of Rose rather than Gypsy Rose Lee, which was why he wrote the book with Rose as the protagonist. Although titled *Gypsy* – a contingency required by Gypsy Rose Lee during the rights acquisition – the plot does not center around the stripper "Gypsy," but rather her vagabond, fame-seeking "gypsy" mother.[3] Arthur Laurents labeled the show as being "suggested by the memoirs of Gypsy Rose Lee" – not "based on" or even "inspired by" the memoirs, but merely "suggested by." The loose connection to the original document was both obvious and intentional, and the writing team's creative license turned the musical into a show that made Rose the star and, even more importantly, one that made her a "madwoman."

The character of Rose in both works constantly walks the fine line between ambition and obsession, between being driven and being mad. In the memoir, she teeters but manages to stay on the "sane" side of the line. In the musical, she crosses that line in a gradual yet definitive leap. My goal in this section is not simply to compare the memoir and the musical, but also to explore the choices that the creators made to alter the original story and analyze the impact of those choices. I center on the following alterations: the addition of music, the invention of the character Herbie, who exists in the musical but not in the memoir, the choice to feature Rose and primarily female characters in almost all the musical numbers, and the notion of female authorship of Rose's character in the performances of Ethel Merman and her successors.

Memoir Rose vs. Musical Rose

Rose's personality in the musical adaptation is almost spot-on to the original memoir. Additionally, her character in the show gleans several other key aspects from the character of the memoir. For example, in the memoir, Rose has "dreams" that reveal ideas for the act – the cow costume, for which Louise plays the "front" in both the memoir and the show, is inspired by Rose's

---

[3] A note on the term "gypsy": this is an appropriated term of the Roma people, and possesses problematic connotations within an appropriative context. I do not use this term descriptively out of respect for its true origins; the only references to the word throughout the document signify the titles of the musical, the memoir, and the chosen stage name of Gypsy Rose Lee. For more information on the appropriated use of this term throughout American theater history, see Paulson (2018).

"dream." This plot point occurs almost verbatim in the musical adaptation. Another example is Rose's love for – or, rather, comic obsession with – animals, which are portrayed as outlandish household pets.

The character catalogue in the show is an abridged version of the memoir's long list of fascinating figures who come in and out of Louise's (and, later, Gypsy's) life. For example, the memoir features a character named F.E. Gorham, a remarkably unscrupulous con-woman whom Rose befriends for a time while touring the act with Louise and June, only to find that F.E. does not have the connections for the act that she claims to have. A darkly funny character, F.E. Gorham possesses too brief a stint in Rose's life to make it into the show. In the memoir, F.E.'s unethical practices make Rose's own small cons pale by comparison, thereby portraying Rose as less atrocious.

Other characters in both narratives differ from source to adaptation, but the most noticeable difference – besides Laurents's invention of Herbie, discussed later in this section – is the character Louise herself. As the autobiographical narrator of the memoir, Louise possesses more feeling and emotional bandwidth than in the show, in which she is timid and likeable. As the musical number "Little Lamb" suggests, young Louise is compliant and gentle. In the memoir, spunky Louise, though also a lover of animals, has more grit and arrogance. The Louise of the show has little personality until her monologue before "Rose's Turn," after becoming "Gypsy Rose Lee." Like June, her character and personality throughout the musical take a backseat to Rose's.

It is important to note that the young Louise of the memoir does not possess any grand acting, dancing, or musical talent absent in Laurents's version; rather, her stage presence in the memoir is remarkably similar to the awkward adolescent of the musical. One recurring musical number mentioned in the memoir – but, sadly, never recreated for the musical – is the number "I'm a Hard-boiled Rose," which Louise sings periodically on tour as part of their ever-failing act. The nonsensical song title says much about young Louise: she is unappetizing and cast-off, yet she is a painstakingly loyal shadow to her mother Rose. The memoir includes a scene between the adult Gypsy and June, in which Gypsy contemplates her life on stage – a realistic moment of reflection omitted from the musical adaptation. June talks of Gypsy's success, and Gypsy retorts, "What successes? . . . I'm a Hard-boiled Rose? That's the only success I can remember. From Hard-boiled Rose to Gypsy Rose – the story of my life" (Lee, 1999: 319). The name "Rose" is, of course, used in a different song title in the musical ("Everything's Coming Up Roses").

The male characters, however secondary to the female characters in the memoir and musical, prove that the show, while focused on Rose first and foremost, holds Louise as a close second, and June as a third. The character

"Pop" in the musical coincides fairly well with "Grandpa" in the memoir. Rose and her daughters live with him at the story's beginning, and Gypsy's book depicts a similarly cantankerous character: someone who would prefer that Rose settle down and allow a more "ladylike" life for her daughters, yet who puts up with her antics without much of a fight. Gypsy explains how "he didn't approve of theatricals, as he put it. Piano lessons, yes. And singing lessons. Those were accomplishments a young lady could display in her own parlor" (Lee, 1999: 9). Although the memoir portrays Rose in disagreement with her father's notions, it features no "Some People" moment for Rose to proudly declare herself as a determined Other. In both, Rose blatantly ignores her father's patriarchal stance.

In terms of the other male characters, both sources discuss Rose's former husbands in passing commentary only, rather than as fleshed-out characters. In both, Rose's previous divorces are portrayed as having been liberating moments, opportunities for Rose and her daughters to live a life not shackled in domesticity and become free to pursue show business, therefore also revealing Rose as living outside the norms of gender roles. In the memoir, Gypsy writes that "June and I never got to know [the husbands] very well. They weren't around long enough … Whenever Mother was married we didn't work; we trouped only between marriages." She goes on to explain how Rose's last husband "accused Mother of not raising us properly" and that as soon as she divorced him "we went back to the stage, this time for good. Mother decided she would never marry again. 'It isn't fair to the children's career,' she said" (Lee, 1999: 13).

As in the musical adaptation, the memoir's Rose uses show business as an excuse to maintain her independence from married life. However, she is not above flirtation and even forming a pseudo-romantic relationship as a method of getting what she wants. Rose has a relationship with an agent named Sam Gordon in the memoir, similar in some ways to Herbie in the show, with whom she aggressively flirts in order to secure his services as their touring agent. Gypsy explains her exasperation with Rose's shameless seduction techniques: "I couldn't look at her … her eyes were too blue, her cheeks too flushed. I'd seen her like that twice before and each time she had married the man" (Lee, 1999: 23). In both the show and the memoir, Rose is not a true romantic, but rather a manipulator of the male partners in her life, because her true priority remains show business.

Even as such, the memoir's Rose is not immune to feelings of attachment and abandonment. One moment reveals Rose in a rare instance of vulnerability – the moment when Sam Gordon leaves when June and Louise are young teenagers. Rose's initial response is fury; she exclaims, "I'll show him. I'll put this act back on the Orpheum Circuit if it's the last thing I do. He'll come crawling back on his hands and knees. Mark my words." However, Gypsy then observes: "Her dry lips began to move and I heard her say, 'I'm going to try and pick up the tangled threads of my life … I'm going to start in all over again,' she said almost to herself, '– alone with my two babies against the world'" (Lee, 1999: 98). This brief glimpse into one of Rose's weaknesses shows an emotional nakedness that is reflected in two moments in the musical: the Act I finale (the number "Everything's Coming Up Roses" and its preceding scene) and in "Rose's Turn."

In "Everything's Coming Up Roses," Rose's confidence in Louise as the act's new headliner comes across as pure delusion. The memoir and the show feature similar scenes in which Rose learns the shocking news of June's elopement. In the memoir, this scene occurs in a hotel in Topeka, Kansas; in the musical, it is set at a train station in Omaha, Nebraska. However, the memoir possesses no moment of dramatic declaration when Rose hears of June's desertion of the family and the act; this part of the scene was added by Laurents as a lead-in to "Everything's Coming Up Roses" and the show's turning point. While Rose is emotional and even frantic as she reads June's note in the memoir, this moment does not directly lead to an announcement of Louise's unrealized talent; rather, it simply serves to further expose Rose's fear of abandonment. Louise, who is perceived as stricken and doubtful in the show, here displays a grimmer opinion of her mother's fate. Rose says, "But [June] has left me – you're all I have now, Louise. Promise me you'll never leave me. Promise me that, dear. Say you'll never leave me!" Gypsy narrates that "[Mother] held my arms tightly and looked hard into my eyes … I knew why my sister had run away and I didn't blame her. If I'd had the chance I would have run, too, as far as I could" (Lee, 1999: 143).

As in the show, Louise does not abandon Rose at this point in the memoir. Rather, she travels home to Seattle with Rose to regroup and gather girls for a whole new act. Louise gradually moves into the star position of the act, rather than being pushed into it by Rose from the moment June leaves. The act is first called "Madam Rose's Dancing Daughters," and Rose, always in denial, fails to concede the act's lack of success. It is Louise herself who suggests that she headline the act, under the new title also heard in the show: "Rose Louise and Her Hollywood Blondes." Parallel to the musical adaptation, the act eventually – and unknowingly – winds up booked in a third-rate burlesque house in the remote city of Wichita, Kansas.

Rose's main shortcoming in both the memoir and the musical is her complete refusal to acknowledge the death of vaudeville. In the memoir, as she gawks at the thought of performing in a burlesque theater, Louise frankly tells her,

"There's no place left for us to work any more [*sic*], Mother. There is no more vaudeville. It doesn't exist any more [*sic*]. If we're going to stay in show business –" Rose interrupts, in a rare moment of self-awareness, "*If?* What are you saying, Louise? Show business is my whole life. I've sacrificed everything for it. What is there for me but show business?" (Lee, 1999: 180). This comment may be what inspired the musical number "Rose's Turn," although that number does not occur until much later in the plot.

The key difference between memoir and adaptation here is Louise's authority within the mother–daughter relationship. In this pivotal moment in the memoir, Louise – not Rose – says to the burlesque theater director, "This is the end for us. But we'll play the week. We need the money," as Rose and the other girls walk silently behind her into the theater (Lee, 1999: 180). Of course, that moment proves to be far from the end, in both versions of the story. But in the memoir, from this moment on, Louise becomes a much larger driving force behind her success as a stripper than she is in the musical adaptation, in which she bows to Rose's choices and does not claim her own achievement until the very end.

In the memoir, once Gypsy finds burlesque success, she buys Rose a farm – a rustic counterpart to the bustling life of the road and the city that Rose knew during her daughter's childhood, and a phase of life that we never witness in the musical adaptation. Rose still calls her daughter on the phone and visits her, but she bows out of Gypsy's career much more gracefully than in the musical. That is not to say Rose becomes graceful, for her character does not undergo such a dramatic change; farm-Rose is not without some feelings of bitterness, for it seems she is incapable of ever being truly satisfied. The following scene from the memoir demonstrates this point perfectly: Rose enters Gypsy's Grammercy Park, New York apartment "carrying a wilted bunch of dahlias, a net shopping bag filled with jars of home-made jelly, and Solly, her favorite rooster, wrapped in a pink baby blanket. Bootsie and Runty, the two poodles, scampered in behind her." She is coming from the farm, and shouts at Gypsy in exasperation, much like the musical's Rose would do: "All we're good for is to work like horses on that farm of yours." Gypsy retorts, "It's your farm. You're the one who wanted it. You're the one who bought it. I'm just the one who paid for it," to which Rose replies, "That's beside the point," and goes on to comment, gossip, and make a scene about nothing important or emotionally deep (Lee, 1999: 279–280).

One brief instance in the memoir highlights Rose's desire, albeit relatively negligible, to receive credit for her daughter's success. Rose calls Gypsy on the phone, infuriated about a newspaper story highlighting a feud (or, as Gypsy explains, a publicity stunt) between Gypsy and June. Rose shouts in her typical hyperbolic fashion,

> I don't ask much of you and your sister, and I certainly know better than to
> expect gratitude for the years I scrubbed and slaved to make stars of you both,
> but I am entitled to a few crumbs of appreciation … It's all right for you girls
> to have a publicity feud, but not at my expense. It makes me look like an
> unnatural mother.

Gypsy replies, "But, you aren't mentioned in the story," and Rose retorts, "That's just it … If anyone deserves to be in a feud with you two girls it's your mother!" (Lee, 1999: 317).

This exchange, though comedic, reveals some of Rose's thoughts that reflect the need for recognition that is so prominently portrayed in the musical. Combined with Rose's earlier comment "show business is my whole life," these aspects may have inspired, to some degree, "Rose's Turn." However, there is no major moment in the memoir that resembles "Rose's Turn" or that portrays Rose's reflection on her entire life as a mother and unsuccessful star in her own right; in short, there is no "mad scene." The addition of this important number featuring Rose at the end of the show truly sets the musical adaptation apart from the memoir, revealing an entirely different purpose for being. Whereas the memoir primarily serves as Gypsy Rose Lee's early life and career story, the musical adaptation is truly a tale about Rose in the middle-aged years of her life, and the psychological toils of being a stage mother who never gets her own spotlight.

What Music Adds to the Story

The most obvious change made by the musical's creators was, of course, the addition of music. The musical adaptation caused alterations in the characters that both simplified and complicated them in different ways. Due to the shorter book and cutting of many scenes and dialogue into a feature-length musical, the characters exist as snapshots, rather than having fully fleshed-out storylines. However, music also allows for character development that cannot exist in the literary medium alone. As Sondheim explains, "In *Gypsy*, all the climaxes of emotion and action erupt into music because they can't go further without it. A good character song does something that *can't* be done by a line by the book writer" (Sondheim, in Zadan, 1989: 42).

Broadly speaking, what Sondheim suggests here is that music can define a character beyond words alone. It allows for the presence of a singing voice, which possesses strong emotive and expressive power. Music provides subtext through melodic themes that reference other characters, emotions, and plot points. It creates tension and resolution through chromaticism, timbre, volume, and many other such musical characteristics. Even though the music in *Gypsy* takes up space that might otherwise be dialogue or monologue, thus prohibiting certain character development, it produces a different, yet more effective, method of showcasing relationships and emotions.

The Invention of Herbie

One of the most notable changes the creators made in adapting the memoir into the musical was the invention of the character Herbie. Throughout the musical, Herbie serves as Rose's foil, the moral compass to her unscrupulous nature. Following the "tragicomedy" style, their relationship is both comedic and serious. At times, Rose's amorality is comically exaggerated while Herbie's morality remains a baseline to which the audience can relate, such as during the number "Small World." At other times, Rose's choices appear to be truly villainous or insane, while Herbie's choices appear heroic and sane.

As argued throughout this Element, Rose is not actually a villain, but rather an anti-hero. Similarly, Herbie is not a "hero," *per se*, but rather he is a "voice of reason" or "moral compass" character – arguably the only one in the show, perhaps besides Pop, who appears only briefly in Act I. Of course, every comparison is relative; some would argue that any person who would spend years partnered with Rose as Herbie does is hardly "moral," but within the show's context, he remains the most relatable character for the audience. In this section, we consider the question: why did the creators of the musical add Herbie to the story? Although Arthur Laurents states that Herbie was the character that he "dreamt up to be [Gypsy Rose Lee]'s mother's lover," (Laurents, 2009: 379) Herbie cannot be defined as the usual type of love interest. As later analysis of "Small World" and "You'll Never Get Away from Me" shows, Rose and Herbie's relationship hardly qualifies as a typical musical theater romantic subplot, exposing one of *Gypsy*'s most notable differences from many other "Golden Age" musicals, such as those of Rodgers and Hammerstein, for which romance is usually a key plot component.[4] *Gypsy* displays almost no romance, not only for Rose, the protagonist, but for all characters. In fact, besides Rose and Herbie, the only other couple in the show is June and Tulsa, who are never seen alone together; Tulsa's "love song" to June, "All I Need is the Girl," is actually sung in Louise's presence, shortly before her sister elopes with him.

Of course, it is important to note here that *Gypsy* was not the first musical to feature such a diversion from the typical romantic style; Larry Stempel claims

---

[4] *The King and I* (1951) by Rodgers and Hammerstein is a prominent exception, as the two protagonists, Anna and the King, do not have a romantic relationship. However, the romantic subplot between Lun Tha and Tuptim remains an important part of the story.

that Lerner and Loewe's 1956 musical *My Fair Lady* was groundbreaking in this regard. He explains how they changed musical conventions when adapting George Bernard Shaw's original play *Pygmalion* – much like the creators of *Gypsy* did when adapting Gypsy Rose Lee's memoir, although their show differs from *My Fair Lady* in many other ways (Stempel, 1992: 142). *Gypsy* instead focuses on the mother–daughter relationship between Rose and Louise. Raymond Knapp explains how "*Gypsy* is – daringly for a musical – about the 'marriage' between mother and daughter, with Herbie functioning as the third leg in the triangle" (Knapp, 2006: 217).

Herbie, although created entirely for the musical, has some basis for inspiration in the memoir. Arthur Laurents recalls that "when [Gypsy Rose Lee] saw the script and read the part about Herbie, the mother's boyfriend, she said, 'God, I wish I had thought of that for my autobiography!'" (Garebian, 1994: 39). The joke here is, of course, that Gypsy Rose Lee's "autobiography" is more novel than memoir, but her book was full of its own fascinating characters on which to base a new one like Herbie. Keith Garebian explains that Herbie's character is "a version of the memoir's Sam Gordon" (Garebian, 1994: 42). Garebian describes Gordon as a "mysterious stranger," which is quite accurate; in the memoir, Louise dislikes him – similar to her distrust of Herbie in the first half of the musical – and finds him unnerving, even creepy. Herbie, however, is almost bland in comparison; he is, according to the stage directions when he first enters in Act I scene 4, "a nice-looking man" with a "sweetly sad, tired quality" (Laurents, 1989: 14). Louise distrusts him because of her loyalty to her mother, but, unlike Gordon, Herbie is kind, and shares nothing of Rose's taste for unscrupulousness.

Herbie remains "sad" and "tired" throughout the musical, growing weaker as Rose's determination grows stronger. His sense of conscience, however, does feebly persist, such as in the scene preceding "You'll Never Get Away from Me," when he criticizes Rose for stealing the silverware from the Chinese restaurant. Throughout Rose's periodic shifts further and further away from morality – or Herbie's version of it, that is – Herbie stands to question her decisions. During the two most important turning points in the plot, he attempts to talk sense into Rose; he appears sane and grounded while Rose seems obsessive. These two moments are the Act I final scene, culminating in "Everything's Coming Up Roses," and Act II scene 3, when Rose sends Louise onto the burlesque stage for her first strip. In this second scene, Herbie leaves Rose in a final show of ethical strength.

In Herbie's final scene, his perspective is complicated; although Herbie does serve as the moral conscience of the "amoral" Rose when the audience witnesses Rose offer her own daughter to dance in the strip act, his voice nonetheless does not win in the end. On the day of their planned wedding, an oblivious and optimistic Herbie exclaims, "I'm finally getting everything I wanted!" (Laurents, 1989: 88). Seconds later, as he watches Rose offer Louise's services for a spot on stage as a burlesque performer – the moment that kick-starts Gypsy Rose Lee's career – he realizes that Rose will never leave show business for him, even if that means entering her daughter into the lowbrow world of burlesque. He claims that he can never marry Rose, telling her that "all the vows from here to doomsday . . . they couldn't make you a wife. I want a wife, Rose. I'm going to be a man if it kills me" (Laurents, 1989: 91).

This final line about "being a man" is interesting, not because of its allowance for masculinity within a female-driven plot, but rather the opposite: it highlights Rose's refusal to let a patriarchal structure dominate her life. In this moment when Herbie leaves for good, the curtain is drawn on Herbie's and Rose's relationship, and the central relationship of the show is finally shown without interruption: the mother–daughter connection between Rose and Louise. This female-focused relationship subverts the heteronormative and sexually forced romantic plotline typical of musicals and allows for a much more nuanced character in Rose. As Stacy Wolf explains, "*Gypsy* eschews heterosexual marriage for a gynocentric world, comes forth as a star vehicle for a single woman's performance, and develops a primary relationship between two women" (Wolf, 2002: 108).

Female Presence and Authorship in *Gypsy*'s Music

Although *Gypsy: A Memoir* and *Gypsy: A Musical Fable* feature the same three female protagonists, the musical *Gypsy* takes this focus a step further. Not only are the majority of the primary characters female, which is unusual for a musical in the mid twentieth-century era (or even in today's era), but almost all of the musical numbers are performed by a female character. While a handful of numbers do include men (Herbie in "You'll Never Get Away from Me" and "Together Wherever We Go" and the chorus boys in June's Act I numbers), the only song that truly features a male character is Tulsa's "All I Need is the Girl." Herbie, originally played by actor Jack Klugman who possessed hardly any singing talent, has little to sing and no solo song of his own; the character is still frequently cast with an actor who lacks strong singing experience. Overall, the dominant presence in *Gypsy*, both in the book and in the score, remains a female one.

In this way, *Gypsy* was ahead of its time, standing out among contemporary musicals. Many other musicals from the mid twentieth century do feature female protagonists, such as Maria in *The Sound of Music*, Eliza in *My Fair*

Lady, and Fanny in *Funny Girl,* just to name a few. However, those all also feature a male protagonist, a male hero figure with a place of importance in the plot and a voice within the score as well. As *Gypsy* includes no major romantic plotline, Herbie's significance lies far behind that of Rose and Louise within the plot and score.

Although *Gypsy* features women so strongly in its music, the musical adaptation shifted the female authorship of the memoir to the primarily male authorship of the show, appropriating – some may argue – Gypsy Rose Lee's female authorial voice. However, opera scholar Carolyn Abbate's notion of authorial voice applies here. She empowers female vocal presence in opera with a critical move away from "the monological authority of 'the Composer,'" arguing that "music is written by a composer, but made and given phenomenal reality by performers" (Abbate, 1991: x).

Remarking on the male gaze, as well as the male authorship of operatic scores, Abbate also references film scholar Laura Mulvey's well-known analysis of male/subject and female/object. Abbate adds, however, that the authorial power of the female *voice* alters this dichotomy within opera. She explains that "visually, the character singing is the passive object of our gaze. But, aurally, she is resonant ... as a voice she slips into the "male/active/subject" position" (Abbate, 1993: 254).

Abbate's bold statement examines the power of the female performer to subvert the male-written plot and music. Additionally, she endows the performer herself – in *Gypsy*'s case, Ethel Merman, or her successors – with a role in the creative process. Numerous female actors throughout the last six decades have portrayed Rose in varying fashions, participating as an author of the character in their own right. In this way, *Gypsy* is, in many important respects, a musical not only primarily sung by women but also partly authored by women. As Arthur Laurents says,

> Every production [of *Gypsy*] is ... going to be different from every other because a different actress is going to be playing Rose, and the production takes its character from her. Visualize Ethel Merman, Angela Lansbury, Tyne Daly, Bernadette Peters, or Patti LuPone as Rose and you know you will see five very different *Gypsy*s. (Laurents, 2009: 16)

A comparison of Ethel Merman to the real-life Rose Hovick, as portrayed in the memoir of Gypsy Rose Lee, speaks to Merman's ability to create a bold character in the original production of *Gypsy*. The greatest praise on this front comes from Gypsy Rose Lee herself, who interviewed Ethel Merman on her talk show, *The Gypsy Rose Lee Show*. Gypsy Rose Lee was present during the show's rehearsal process, and after observing Merman's performance she stated, "It was during these rehearsals that I realized that Ethel was really more like Mother than I thought she was. She had Mother's energy, her resourcefulness, most of all her wonderful sense of humor" (Lee, 1967).

Ethel Merman came to the cast of *Gypsy* as an established, well-known Broadway performer, known for the brassy timbre of her voice and her staunch, stand-and-belt, showstopping numbers. She was a vocal innovator on Broadway; Mark N. Grant describes her voice as being "highly unusual in not being dusky but rather bright and almost a spinto soprano in timbre – in a word, brassy … her singing sounded like speech yet was carried by well-shaped, clearly intoned pitches" (Grant, 2004: 38). Merman's belt became a type of virtuosity emblematic of female Broadway singers. Reporter Frank Aston describes her voice, drawing on June's recollection of Rose:

> Can you recall the steel-mill timbre of the Merman tootle? As you do so, listen to Miss June: "Mother had a wonderful vocal range … Her speech was vibrant and sent chills up and down your spine. Her fury was like the booming of a cannon. She could be heard half way [*sic*] down the block." (Aston, 1959)

This virtuosity gives authorial weight to Merman's presence on stage in her role as Rose, according to Abbate's theoretical stance on vocal resonance and the singer's authorial voice.

Played by multiple performers over the decades, Rose has seen highly different interpretations in terms of the grandiosity of her character, including her "madness," particularly in "Rose's Turn." Merman's version was, arguably, not as "mad" as the creators, especially Laurents, intended, thus reclaiming some of the male-written madness in Rose's character in favor of a typical Merman lead character. Keith Garebian quotes Arthur Laurents, who recalled this conversation he had with Merman when discussing her possible involvement in the project:

> [Laurents:] "I want to do a show, but I don't want to do the usual Ethel
>   Merman musical."
> "Neither do I," retorted the actress.
> "This woman [Rose] is a monster. How far are you willing to go?"
> "As far as you want me to … Nobody's ever given me the chance before."
> (Garebian, 1994:35–36)

In his interviews and memoirs, however, Laurents criticizes what he considers Merman's lack of acting skills. In *Original Story By,* he says that "she did her best and was hailed for being her best but Ethel Merman was a voice, a presence, and a strut, not an actress" (Laurents, 2000: 378).

Sondheim possesses a higher opinion of Merman's acting skills than Laurents, although even Sondheim hints that her performance not as astounding as some reviewers make her out to be. In his notes on "Everything's Coming Up Roses" in *Finishing the Hat*, he explains that Merman had

> never been tested as an actress. We had no reason to believe she could do anything but bray her way through the show … As it happened, Ethel turned out to be a better actress than we'd anticipated, limited in range but capable of shadings and variety and with, of course, impeccable timing. She was able to tap into the reserve of anger that fuels every comedian, high or low. (Sondheim, 2011: 67–68)

Although Ethel Merman's acting never met the full approval of some of *Gypsy*'s creative team, critics largely touted her praises, happily surprised at this "new" Ethel Merman. For example, Jack Gaver writes: "It's no joke to Ethel Merman that, after 13 musical shows and 30 stage years, she is suddenly hailed as an 'actress' instead of just as an easy-does-it comedienne who can belt a song like nobody else" (Graver, 1959). Richard Watts Jr. similarly paints Merman's acting in a positive light, touting her ability to display Rose's "human" characteristics:

> There is nothing sentimental about the characterization of the driving and implacable woman who devoted her life to a determination to make stars of her two unwilling daughters, and succeeded in driving both of them to revolt. The mother of the girls named June and Louise is shown as completely selfish, merciless and unceasing in her efforts to dominate her helpless children, and the only thing that keeps her from being a monster is her unconquerable and zestful spirit and Miss Merman's gift for making her both human and a little touching. (Watts, 1959)

Another reviewer, Thomas R. Dash, describes:

> As the possessive mother who is bent on making her two little girls stars, who scrimps, scrounges and browbeats everyone that gets into her way, Miss Merman is a whirlwind of energy. As the domineering mother with this monomaniac passion for her daughter's stardom, Miss Merman offers a wonderful delineation of a woman who is almost a monster. (Dash, 1959)

In the first Broadway revival of *Gypsy*, however, Angela Lansbury's interpretation of Rose, co-created by Laurents himself as the production's director, displayed a more elevated, and perhaps "madder," version of the character. Through her acting, Lansbury differentiated her version of Rose from that of Ethel Merman – not in an effort to outdo Merman, but to provide a new angle to the character and to the revival of *Gypsy* as a whole. Lansbury herself compares her performance to Merman's, explaining that

> The original Rose was not an actress … so she was singing about herself. That's OK; we all bring slices of ourselves to Rose. What I brought was my total understanding of the character, as a character actress, which I think perhaps I was more so than any of the other ladies who've played it. For me, she was a whole character, that's what I brought, my understanding of this human. (Lansbury, in Peikert, 2020)

Laurents explains, "Because [Angela Lansbury] was a marvelous actress, I wanted to direct this *Gypsy*: with Angie, it would be a very different play with very different values, one much closer to the play I had written" (Laurents, 2000: 395). The "humanness" of Lansbury's Rose does not contradict the notion of a "madder" Rose than Merman's; rather, it emphasizes it. While grand and operatic, Rose's madness can also be interpreted as a real, human mental condition.

Other performers have brought their own authorial voice to Rose's character on stage over the last six decades, with varying degrees of "madness" sewn into the role.[5] None have taken the role quite as psychologically far as Imelda Staunton, who performed the role of Rose in the first West End revival of *Gypsy* in 2015. According to critic Matt Trueman, Sondheim himself suggested Staunton for the role in *Gypsy*. Staunton's Rose was enormously well received, as critics and audiences seemed to respond positively to her harsh, ruthless take on the character (Trueman, 2015).

Critical reviews of Imelda Staunton's performance depict her as an impressively menacing Rose who takes the character's monstrousness to new heights. Michael Billington went so far as to laud how "every facet of the character [Rose] is caught by Imelda Staunton who gives one of the greatest performances I've ever seen in musical theater" (Billington, 2015). Staunton's Rose is gruff, rough around the edges, and intimidating, pushing the boundaries of the character's mental instability further than any performer in a major production of *Gypsy* had before. Susannah Clapp describes her performance pointedly, stating that

> as Momma Rose Imelda Staunton enters like a female Napoleon. Her walk is beetling; she hits the words of her songs like a terrier shaking a rat. She is the hellish quintessence of a stage mother, a magnified version of any woman who has sapped her child's energy by her own superior vitality and the force of her own need … Staunton gets the gusto, the ruthlessness and the pathos. (Clapp, 2014)

---

[5] Following Merman's original rendition of the character, Rose has been performed on Broadway and film by: Rosalind Russell (1962 film), Angela Lansbury (1973 West End premiere and 1974 Broadway revival), Tyne Daly (1989 Broadway revival), Bette Midler (1993 television film), Bernadette Peters (2003 Broadway revival), Patti LuPone (2008 Broadway revival), Imelda Staunton (2015 West End revival), and Audra McDonald (2024 Broadway revival).

In a similar vein, critic Leslie Felperin writes that Staunton's Rose is "petite and pugnacious … a yapping, growling mutt: half terrier like the Yorkie tucked under her arm, half pitbull" (Felperin, 2015). Matt Trueman calls her a "gutsy little gumball of a woman … a drill sergeant, a mega-fan, a cult leader and even, yes, a mother" (Trueman, 2015).

Compared to Merman and Lansbury, Staunton proves that female madness can be molded and subverted into an intense psychological display – one that leaves the audience in fascinated horror. Simultaneously fearing and pitying her madness, we are left to decide if this display is powerful or victimizing – or, as McClary argues, somewhere in between: a martyrdom, as Rose's spirit dies to the patriarchal structures at play in her life.

3 Rose's Musical Numbers

The "I had a dream" Motive

The most important leitmotif and signifier of Rose's progressive madness throughout *Gypsy*'s score is the "I had a dream" motive. Introduced in the overture, first sung in "Some People," and featured in both "Everything's Coming Up Roses" and "Rose's Turn," this motive symbolizes Rose's delusions – her "dreams" – the plot element that serves as the crux of her madness.

The motive's first two appearances in the score, at the beginning and the end of the overture, foreshadow the finale of the musical. Its place at the end of the overture is particularly interesting; a deceptive ending occurs featuring the music of the number "Mr. Goldstone, I Love You" but then pivots to "I had a dream" for the final cadential moment – a much more fitting ending from the perspective of plot importance (Sondheim & Styne, 1959, Original Broadway Cast Recording [OCR], track 1, 4'29").

The "I had a dream" motive, appearing in numerous keys throughout the musical, maintains the simple sol-do-sol-re intervallic structure. Its melody is soaring, recognizable, and tonal – full of hope. As it does not represent Rose's excess in any chromatic or musically outstanding way, it instead serves to alert the audience to her delusional state through its repetition and, eventually, the blatant irony of its hopeful sound, as Rose's own hopes spiral out of her grasp throughout the course of the musical.

The motive's rhythmic structure is likewise not complex, but the triplet half notes in the melody do possess a subtle pull of obstinate difference against the quarter note chords in the accompaniment, representing Rose's tendency to stand apart in her fight for her dreams. Raymond Knapp posits that the triplet basis of the motive is important in the overall theme of the show:

> The deployment of triplets within a duple meter will form its own core of
> motivic development across the show, evolving first as a setting for idealist
> inspiration tinged with a certain cheapness (a visual archetype for Broadway
> itself) that will eventually degenerate into the bump-and-grind triplets of the
> burlesque hall. (Knapp, 2006: 221)

The frequent repetition of Rose's "dreams" in her music also alerts the audience to a type of interjection that goes beyond Rose's traits of determination and gumption and into the realm of madness. As Joseph Straus explains, a frequent manifestation of madness in musical contexts is the hearing of voices, often represented musically through repeated quotations (Straus, 2018: 94). Rose hears "voices" or sees visions through her dreams, and the "I had a dream" motive signifies those voices; every time she repeats the motive, a bit of madness appears in her actions.

It is important to note that the "I had a dream" motive is also recurrently imitated in the orchestra after Rose sings it, making the motive more prominent and pervasive in the audience's ear. For example, after Rose first sings the motive in "Some People," she expounds the aspects of her "dream" and then, in the accompaniment, the motive appears in various instruments one after the other – first the violins, then trumpets, followed by oboe, and finally piccolo. Table 1 indicates all significant appearances of the "I had a dream" motive.

Rose's "I Want" Song: "Some People"

Rose's opening number "Some People" in Act I scene 2 introduces *Gypsy*'s main character to the audience by defining her motives, her dreams (or, rather, delusions), and the lengths to which she will go to accomplish them. In this number, Rose immediately and definitively Otherizes herself to the audience. She loudly proclaims she is not "some people"; she believes that she is different, better, and stronger than the rest of the world. This number fits what is commonly known in musical theater as the "I Want" song: an early number in a show that reveals a character's desires and driving forces and launches their journey in the plot.

In this number and its preceding scene, Rose arrives at her father's Seattle home after their local audition. Determined to "make it" in vaudeville, Rose decides to leave Seattle in pursuit of this dream – but first, she needs money. Her "Pop" possesses an old gold retirement plaque – worth eighty-eight dollars, he tells Rose – and Rose attempts to manipulate him into giving it to her. The lyrics of "Some People" include both Rose's sung monologue and her speech to her father. Pop's role in this scene is that of the voice of reason. The stage directions,

Table 1 "I had a dream" motive occurrences and significances

Musical number	Measure	Key	Signifiers of Rose's madness
Overture	mm. 1–2	E-flat Major	Foreshadowing the show's overall theme of madness, these are the first notes the audience hears
Overture	mm. 228–229	B-flat Major	Foreshadowing the show's ending and Rose's mad scene, "Rose's Turn" (ends in dominant key of overture's starting key)
"Some People"	mm. 75–76	F Major	First "dream": "All about June and the Orpheum Circuit" – signifies Rose's delusion
"Some People"	mm. 87–88	E-flat Major	Reiteration of first dream
"Some People"	mm. 115–116	F Major	Second reiteration of first dream, this time with manipulation/ monetary incentive: "And all that I need/ is eighty-eight bucks" – signifies Rose's unscrupulousness, foreshadowing her greed for success that leads to Rose pushing Louise into burlesque
"Everything's Coming Up Roses"	mm. 3–4	E-Flat Major	Foreshadowing Rose having yet another delusional "dream" as the song begins; motive indicates Rose is becoming madder through her performance of this number

Table 1 (cont.)

Musical number	Measure	Key	Signifiers of Rose's madness
Incidental Music (Act II scene 4) (not on OCR)	mm. 38–39	E-flat Major	Occurs right after Rose claims "But let's walk away a star!" as she pushes Louise to perform her first strip and Herbie walks out. Foreshadows Louise's success and the events leading up to "Rose's Turn"
"Rose's Turn"	mm. 95–96	D Major	- Rose declares she dreamed her dreams for June, Herbie, and Louise - Followed by statement "Don't I get a dream for myself?" - Moment in which Rose's dreams no longer serve her; she subconsciously realizes the madness of it all
"Rose's Turn"	mm. 140–142 (different rhythm, spread out over two iterations of "For me!")	A Major	- First 4 iterations of "for me!" on sol-do - Final iteration of "for ME!" on sol-re - Rose finally descends fully into the madness of her narcissism

when he enters, state that "He is a crusty old man, holding the Bible he is eternally reading" (Laurents, 1989: 9). The Bible prop, a seemingly minute detail, establishes Pop's character as a foil to Rose's; he is someone who "lives by the Book," grounded in a socially acceptable belief system.

Pop reveals his daughter's character flaws when Rose herself refuses to acknowledge them. He says, "You oughta be ashamed: fooling your kids with those dreams!" Rose replies, "They're real dreams and I'm gonna make 'em *come* real for my kids!" Pop calls her a "crazy woman" – foreshadowing, perhaps, the trajectory that begins here and ends with Rose's mad scene. Pop then claims, "It ain't too late for you to get a husband to support you." Rose, never the domestic housewife, admits, "After three husbands, I'm through with marriage. I want to enjoy myself. I want my girls to enjoy themselves and travel like Momma does!" (Laurents, 1989: 10–11). Here, Pop establishes a standard that becomes a major element of the storytelling in *Gypsy*: that of the male moral compass. He is the first male character in the show to serve as the voice of reason, trying – and failing – to divert Rose from her schemes.

In the dialogue between Pop and Rose that occurs before and during "Some People," Pop points out three aspects of Rose's character that set her apart as an Other figure, both within the plot and within the larger context of a male-dominated society. The first is her "dreams," referring both to her life's aspirations and to her literal dreams, which Rose claims throughout the show to be prophetic, foretelling the success of the children's act. Pop exposes the foolishness of Rose's dreams, causing the audience to see her character's tendency toward delusion.

Rose's references to dreams may be the most obvious display of her pretense, although they appear to be, in her mind, quite literal. For example, in the lyrics of "Some People," Rose describes a "dream" she had in which she meets "Mr. Orpheum" – a delusion, because no such eponymous man existed in association with the famous vaudeville Orpheum circuit. Rose describes her "dream" in the lyrics: "I had a dream/ Just as real as can be, Poppa!/ There I was in Mr. Orpheum's office" (Laurents, 1989: 13–14). As Rose is trying to convince her father, the underlying possibility remains that she knows very well that her "dreams" are not real; she fabricates them to manipulate her listener. However, as Rose's "dreams" reappear several times during major turning points in the musical's plot, they should not be discounted in this scene; Rose often truly does appear to believe them and makes life choices based on their so-called revelations – regardless of their validity.

The second "problem" that Pop reveals about Rose is her lack of a husband. This facet of Rose's character becomes a recurring issue throughout the play, as she forms a relationship with Herbie, whom she refuses to marry. Rose's choice to remain an autonomous woman without, as Pop says, "a husband to support" her, Otherizes her within an early to mid twentieth-century setting in which a woman would rarely stand apart from a male spouse.

Thirdly, Pop questions Rose's ability to be a good mother. Rose's bitterness surrounding her own mother's abandonment, which Pop mentions in the penultimate line of the dialogue preceding "Some People," fuels Rose's desire to create a different path for her own daughters while also contributing to her complicated notions regarding "good" motherhood and parenting. Rose's identity confusion surrounding motherhood partially serves as her impetus for singing "Rose's Turn" at the end of the play, when Louise no longer needs her and Rose reveals that her own motivations were selfish all along, and that she has been, in some ways, a "bad" mother – although a feminist theoretical perspective allows for a more nuanced interpretation of what constitutes "good" or "bad" mothering.[6]

Rose's motivations during "Some People" are not always clear, however. She repeatedly asserts that her motivations are purely for her daughters' sake. "It ain't for me," she claims – but she contradicts this message blatantly, as shown in the following lyrics with the frequent repetition of the word "I," which is also emphasized in the music, with each reiteration occurring on the syncopated beat: "But I at least gotta try/ When I think of all the sights that I gotta see/ And all the places I gotta play/ All the things that I gotta be at/ Come on, Poppa, what'ya say?" (OCR 1959, track 3, 0'47"). However, in the undertones of Rose's dreams for her own success through her daughters, she does display the true and admirable desire to provide them with a life free of the shackles of dependence on men. Another problem with Rose's dream for her daughters, however, lies in its execution. While both June and Louise later prove that they value autonomy from their mother, Rose's inability to let them be independent as adolescents eventually leads to her own downfall, beginning with her response to June's abandonment of her in "Everything's Coming Up Roses" and ending with her reaction to Louise's success in "Rose's Turn."

Rose's refusal to listen to Pop, a patriarchal figure, garners some admiration. However, Rose's manipulation skills, especially with men, both villainize her and outline her excess. At the end of "Some People," Rose fails to convince her father and ends up stealing the plaque off the wall, proving that she has no qualms regarding amoral behaviors such as theft, and possesses no loyalty to him. Herein lies an example of Rose's complicated nature: while she fights tooth and nail for a better life for herself and her daughters, she resorts to stealing in order to achieve her goals. Perhaps she is a monster, or perhaps she is a sort of feminist Robin Hood, robbing the patriarchy to feed the young women who live under her care.

"Some People" also illustrates Rose's complex representation in music. Styne's themes within "Some People" are some of the most important within *Gypsy* as a whole. The music of this number is intense; it jarringly juxtaposes frenetic, climbing, and repetitive melodic lines with soaring,

---

[6] See *"Bad" Mothers* by Molly Ladd-Taylor and Lauri Umansky (1998).

declamatory lines. Rose's opening vocal melody, however, begins surprisingly – on a low-register G-sharp – in an awkward transition from the speaking cue that precedes the musical entrance, in which Rose shouts to Pop, "Fightin' to get up and get out!" (OCR 1959, track 3, 0'14"). Sondheim provides a long explanation in *Finishing the Hat* of the compositional process involved in writing Rose's opening notes. He claims not to have noticed the "anticlimactic thud of this cue until the show was in its Philadelphia tryout" when he heard the number with orchestral accompaniment for the first time. He explains how the song's opening is inconsistent with the character, because "lowering her voice at the peak of passion is something neither Rose nor Merman would ever do." He recalls that he and Styne wrote a traditional verse at the top of the song in which Rose tells Pop to go to hell – but Merman "refused to sing it because, she claimed, her fans would never forgive her for cursing her father. And there the cue to the song sits" (Sondheim, 2011: 60). Paul Laird, in his book on *Gypsy*'s orchestration, explains how proof of this change can be seen in the orchestration manuscripts as well (Laird, 2022: 275).

Sondheim adds a characterization comment after his anecdote about cutting Rose's cursing line, stating that "Rose didn't care what people thought of her; Merman did" (Sondheim, 2011: 60). "Some People" proves that Rose truly does not regard the "sane" opinions of Pop or anyone who comes between her and success. The music of this number – irrespective of its awkward opening notes – repeatedly showcases Rose's gumption. Certain aspects of the harmony reflect this as well; that first low G# occurs as the dissonant augmented fourth of a D minor chord. The next iteration of the word "some," also on a low G# in measure 9, is an augmented second of an F major chord. These dissonances contrast with the following section, in which more consonant harmonies make the number almost feel inspirational, such as the simple 4-3 suspension on the word "I" in measure 33. The melody of Rose's line "But I at least gotta try" soars in a fashion that elicits a feeling of fortitude found in the concept of the American Dream (OCR 1959, track 3, 0'47"). Underneath Rose's triumphant-sounding "I" and "try," each of which last for two and one-half measures, the strings play a sweeping, chromatic melisma that mimics Rose's own bubbling determination.

In the next line, Rose's accompaniment suddenly becomes bare and her singing recitative-like, as she stands practically alone with her quickly forming plans (OCR 1959, track 3, 0'55"). Here she frenetically sings: "When I think of all the sights that I gotta see yet,/ All the places I gotta play,/ All the things that I gotta be yet,/ Hey L.A. I'm comin' your way!" After this section, the momentum shifts as the tempo slows, the accompaniment remains bare, and Rose sings the show's most important leitmotif, the "I had a dream" motive (OCR 1959, track 3, 1'30").

Rose finishes the number with a repeat of the opening music, with newly impassioned lyrics. Rose's goal in the final part of "Some People" is to assert, in multiple reiterations, that she is an Other, she is narcissistically and unapologetically "Rose." She triumphantly self-aggrandizes this notion in the number's final lyrics, holding out a long, belting note on the syllable of her own name: "Well they can stay and rot – / But not Rose!" (OCR 1959, track 3, 3'30").

Rose's Non-Love Songs: "Small World" and "You'll Never Get Away from Me"

"Small World"

The Act I scene 4 number "Small World," Rose's second song, resembles a typical love-at-first-sight number from a "Golden Age" musical in terms of its placement within the act, its role in the plot, and its musical style. However, this number stands out as strikingly different from this surface-level categorization as a love song for several notable reasons; instead, it is better classified as being what Larry Stempel coins a "non-love" song (Stempel, 1992: 142). "Small World" subverts the romance convention in order to create an uncanny experience for the audience – one in which they observe a "love song," but witness no romance from Rose's perspective.

"Small World" is Rose's song to Herbie, whom she first meets in this scene. While it is obvious that Rose is pulling Herbie's heartstrings in this number, her true motivations lie very close beneath the surface. Analysis of the lyrics, as well as consideration of Rose's and Herbie's relationship throughout the musical, reveals how "Small World" is a manipulation song, in which Rose lures Herbie into working for her under the guise of forming a romantic connection. The lyrics contain the subtext of coincidence – a typical "meet cute" in a romantic scenario – but frame a more pragmatic relationship in Rose's one-track, success-driven mind. Herbie embodies everything Rose is not: kind, generous, honest. As a foil to Rose, Herbie exposes Rose's narcissism – a dichotomy that recurs throughout *Gypsy* but that is first witnessed here in "Small World."

The entirety of the song's lyrics consists of Rose describing the "coincidental" commonalities between herself and Herbie. Prior to the number, Herbie indicates a romantic interest in Rose when he helps her get her act booked and asks if she would "consider marrying again." Rose declines, saying: "I like you – but I don't want marriage. You like me – but you don't want show business." Herbie replies, "That seems to leave you there – and me here." Rose, always the opportunist, quips, "Oh, that depends on how you look at it.

You look at what we don't have, I look at what we do have" (Laurents, 1989: 16). After the number, Herbie agrees to manage the act – but Rose does not agree to marriage. Clearly, the song proves to work in Rose's favor.

This non-love song foreshadows the lack of a true romantic plot between Rose and Herbie throughout the musical. Although they maintain a partnership and eventually even plans of marriage until partway through Act II, when Herbie leaves her, there is no clear assertion of a developing love story between them. This absence is reinforced by Rose's and Herbie's other two songs: their duet "You'll Never Get Away from Me" and their trio with Louise "Together Wherever We Go."

Musically, "Small World" fits the typical style of a romance number, adding to the uncanny, and often comedic, listening experience of this non-love song. Opposing the ear-assaulting tempos and loud orchestrations of Rose's "Some People" and Baby June's "Let Me Entertain You" that occur prior to this number (as heard on the original cast recording), "Small World" has a slow, deliberate tempo and minimal orchestration that features high winds and strings (OCR 1959, track 4). Accompanying a brash voice like Ethel Merman's, the musical lightness of this number feels purposely ill-fitting, revealing Rose's insincere motivations behind the romantic lyrics and melody.

Stylistically, "Small World" is a ballad, in a simple AABA form, with an additional BA coda after a small dialogue interlude. The eight-measure phrase of the A section is repetitive with a lilting, pleasant melody. This melody features a relatively narrow and low vocal range that maintains the song's easygoing feeling. The B section barely expands from this light mood, but the addition of chromaticism creates a momentary reflection of Rose's desperation. As she sings, "We have so much in common/ It's a phenomenon," her melody is rife with accidentals that briefly deviate from the B-major key and expose her seductiveness and manipulation (OCR 1959, track 4, 0'57"). This treatment continues into the next phrase.

On the original cast recording, the entire number is sung by Rose alone; in many performances, however, including the original stage performance, Herbie joins in for the coda (Laird, 2022: 164). Regardless, "Small World" remains largely a "Rose" number; it reveals how Rose possesses the upper hand in her relationship with Herbie from the outset. On the one hand, it demonstrates that Rose has a "soft" side; its carefree tempo, simple melody, repetitive phrases, and romantic ballad style reveal a rarely seen part of Rose's typically boisterous and loud personality. On the other hand, however, it also illustrates her cunning, and her character's subversion of musical romantic conventions.

Of course, missing from the libretto, score, and cast recordings of *Gypsy* is the audience response. "Small World" and its previous scene actually include quite a bit of humor, and live performances prove how much the audience laughs throughout Rose's deception. The sarcasm, flirtation, and blatant manipulation from Rose in "Small World" comes across as quite literally "funny." Thus, the underlying darkness of Rose's character that this number reveals is often hidden beneath the surface-level humor, but the seeds are nonetheless sown for interpreting Rose's character development.

"You'll Never Get Away from Me"

The next number that paints Rose as manipulative is the duet with Herbie from Act I entitled "You'll Never Get Away from Me." The title alone reveals Rose's incessant determination to keep people close only so that they can help her accomplish her dreams. This attribute showcases her excessive desires and refusal to admit to the reality of her relationships. Although this song is not overly important to the establishment of Rose's character, a brief analysis of its content does aid in understanding her motivations and actions, especially regarding her relationship with Herbie.

The duet involves Rose and Herbie at an early turning point in the show – not as major as the turning point at the end of Act I, but a foreshadowing of it. Prior to this number, Herbie successfully books an audition for the act on the Orpheum Circuit (as heard in the number "Mr. Goldstone, I Love You"). In the next scene, just before the duet, Herbie and Rose argue about the nature of their relationship; Herbie wants marriage and a commitment from Rose that will give him a reason to stay with her and continue traveling with the act. Rose wants Herbie to keep managing the act but puts off her promise of marriage yet again. He claims that he loves her, but states that someday, he will likely leave her. Knowing the manipulative power she holds over him, Rose uses this song not to argue that she loves him back, but to claim that he cannot escape her; of course, the lyrics also show how Rose is in denial, thinking her influence over Herbie is unassailable, which his walkout in Act II scene 4 eventually disproves.

"You'll Never Get Away from Me" is a short number, and basically consists of Herbie stating he will leave and Rose repeating the number's titular words in various iterations. According to Sondheim, the number – a "trunk song" from Styne's collection of tunes – was just a "jaunty romantic ballad," but of course, that concept takes on a unique meaning when Rose is involved (Sondheim, 2011: 64). The music is "jaunty," yes; it is upbeat and jovial, and, disregarding the number's subtext, sounds like a happy little love song from the moment the opening motive plays in the winds (OCR 1959, track 8, 0'02"). But the lyrics reveal a more menacing undertone not present in the lively music – a clever juxtaposition of appearance and reality.

Sondheim's lyrics depict the sheer determination that Rose exhibits time and time again, as shown in Rose's first verse: "You'll never get away from me./ You can climb the tallest tree,/ I'll be there somehow./ True, you could say, "Hey, here's your hat,"/ But a little thing like that/ Couldn't stop me now." Repetitive melodic lines reveal her unwavering attitude and undeserved certainty in Herbie's attachment to her. Herbie then enters the duet with a new melody (OCR 1959, track 8, 1'05"). Unlike Rose in her first verse, however, Herbie does not sing an uninterrupted section of lyrics in order to fully explain his feelings. Rose interrupts him repeatedly from his second line onward. She continuously pushes him to "shut up and dance" with her in an effort to distract him. The final verse, sung in unison by both, returns to Rose's A section music, proving that Rose's melody – and her argument – wins over Herbie's in the end (OCR 1959, track 8, 1'40").

"You'll Never Get Away from Me" exposes Rose's errant belief in her own truth and no one else's. Her refusal to concede that anyone would leave her eventually leads to breakdown after breakdown, as seen with June's elopement and Rose's response in "Everything's Coming Up Roses," her reaction to Herbie's eventual departure in the cut number "Who Needs Him?" or its replacement "Small World (Reprise)," and of course, her final mad scene, "Rose's Turn."

Rose's Feminist Addendum: "Who Needs Him?" (Cut Number)

Although her non-love songs "Small World" and "You'll Never Get Away from Me" reveal a great deal about her lack of interest in romance, the number "Who Needs Him?" exposes a more vulnerable side of Rose: her fear of abandonment. This fear ultimately becomes the largest contributing factor in her downturn toward madness in "Rose's Turn." Were "Who Needs Him?" left in the show, it would serve as Rose's final turning point in her step toward this downturn. Unfortunately, it does not remain in the score, but can be heard on the 2008 recording with Patti LuPone (OCR 2008, track 25). Only 1:16 long, this number packs a punch in a short amount of time.

Sondheim explains that "Who Needs Him?" was cut because of show length concerns, stating that "this moment was accomplished more economically by a couple of halting lines in a brief reprise of 'Small World'" (Sondheim, 2011: 74). However, the time difference between "Who Needs Him?" and the "Small World" reprise is only about thirty seconds, proving that the switch hardly solved a timing issue. The cut is an unfortunate loss at a crucial moment in the show, as the brief reprise of "Small World" makes Rose appear rather unfazed by Herbie's walkout, which is simply not the case. "Who Needs Him?" reveals that Rose is very disturbed by his abandonment – a revelation that, perhaps, the creators wished to exclude – but her disturbed feelings here indeed match her character based on comments she has made before about her disdain for people walking out on her. This number also reflects her borderline-mad responses to those walkouts, particularly June's at the end of Act I, which is further analyzed in the following section on "Everything's Coming Up Roses." Rose first mentions this fear in Act I scene 2, the scene preceding "Some People." Pop chides that Rose will abandon her daughters, as her own mother abandoned her, to which Rose vehemently shouts, "Never!" (Laurents, 1989: 11). Clearly, loyalty is extremely important to Rose, even if she does not demonstrate her own loyalty successfully because her show business goals always take priority over her personal relationships.

The entire mood of both the lyrics and music of "Who Needs Him?" is one of bitter, sarcastic indignation. Angry at Herbie but still focused on the act's success, Rose pretends not to care that he has left, and she keeps her fear and disappointment well hidden under a shell of strength and independence. In the first verse, she begins singing forcefully over a lamenting string and English horn accompaniment, practically spitting the lyrics, "Who needs him?/ One up, one down" (OCR 2008, track 25, 0'02"). Her emotions flip between anger and despair. Here, Rose's complicated nature reveals itself; while throughout the show she may primarily use Herbie for his management skills rather than romantic partnership, as discussed in analysis of her non-love songs, Rose nonetheless does fall for him in her own way, enough to eventually agree to marry him and even admit that she loves him. Thus, the audience sees through her tough façade enough to know that Rose is indeed heartbroken that Herbie leaves, not for the failed marriage prospect so much as for the abandonment by yet another close person in her life.

Even more importantly, this number reveals more of Rose's thoughts about her past relationships with men. It does not provide specifics, but hints at the coming and going of men in Rose's life throughout the years, and how Rose considers them to be "passing phases" upon whom she does not depend. The implication is that Rose needs only herself – a lonely yet individualistic concept, though spawned by the disappointment Rose has felt at the hands of too many loved ones in her life, especially her own mother and her daughter June. In the second verse of the number, Rose cries, "Who needs him?/ Not me – oh no!/ There will be others to come,/ Sure, and others to go./ They're passing phases./ They can go to blazes!" Musically, this dramatic section builds slowly; Rose sings the first four lines in an almost recitative-like style, with minimal accompaniment and spoken-word style rhythms that reflect her inner dialogue (OCR 2008, track 25, 0'33"). The music of the last two lines then intensifies significantly, climbing stepwise melodically with increasing volume and elongated rhythmic values (OCR 2008, track 25, 0'49").

Rose's music continues to build, then slowly declines in the words of her final coda, "Who needs them?/ Who needs it?/ Who needs him?/ Who? (OCR 2008, track 25, 0'58"). This repetition makes her sound increasingly distraught, accompanied by incrementally decreasing orchestration in each phrase, changes one word at a time, revealing a fascinating feminist breakdown: Rose does not need "them" – her husbands, "it" – the patriarchy, or "him" – Herbie specifically. Although she makes this courageous claim, the repetition also makes her appear unhinged and vulnerable – the last musical step toward the madness witnessed in her next and final number "Rose's Turn."

The Daughters' Perspectives: "Momma's Talkin' Soft" (Cut Number) and "If Momma Was Married"

Two numbers in *Gypsy*, not sung by Rose but by her daughters, provide a vital perspective on Rose's character and aspects of her madness. The cut number "Momma's Talkin' Soft" and the song "If Momma Was Married" serve as the sisters' only duets, and both songs possess the sole thematic subject: their mother.

"Momma's Talkin' Soft"

The cut number "Momma's Talkin' Soft," sung by young June and Louise, originally occurred in Act I scene 4 and played in counterpoint to "Small World." The counterpoint number, though omitted from the original Broadway recording and score, was finally recorded for the 2008 Broadway cast album featuring Patti LuPone, providing an invaluable listening opportunity for analysis. Sondheim claims that "Momma's Talkin' Soft" was not cut for content reasons, but rather because it added too much to the show's length and because the creators ran into hiccups during rehearsals. Although this song was cut from the show, it remains important in this analysis because of its quotation in "Rose's Turn," as well as its relevance in analyzing the character of Rose.

Sondheim also claims that "My only regret about the cut is that I had used fragments of it in the climactic number of the show, 'Rose's Turn,' as you'll see, and their resonance was lost" (Sondhcim, 2011: 60). He later goes on to say, "I couldn't remove the section [in "Rose's Turn"] without collapsing the whole number. So there it remains, with the audience missing the reference. And I regret to say that it doesn't matter" (Sondheim, 2011: 77). However, the argument can be made that it *does* matter – not so much for the plot, but rather for the painting of Rose's character. This song exposes even more about the predatory nature of Rose's relationships. While Rose's own behavior is fully displayed in her musical numbers with Herbie, "Momma's Talkin' Soft" explores her daughters' perspectives and reveals that Rose's manipulative tactics are not specific to Herbie but rather represent a long-existing character trait that her daughters have frequently witnessed with other men over the years.

Sung during her daughters' disturbingly pointed, voyeuristic observation of their mother's initial flirtation with Herbie in "Small World," "Momma's Talkin' Soft" paints Rose as villainous, more so than any number in the show until "Rose's Turn." As such, it foreshadows the monstrosity of her mad scene. As Sondheim explains, part of this cut number sounds in "Rose's Turn," but the quotation is arguably rather more of a lyrical reference – but a poignant one, nonetheless. Like in "Rose's Turn," the music of "Momma's Talkin' Soft" repeats the phrase "Momma's ___" in various iterations, but the melody is different (OCR 2008, track 22, 2'02"). In June and Louise's version, a rhythmically upbeat, sing-song melody comically juxtaposes their haunting lyrics.

The girls sing two full verses before a short interlude and the counterpoint with "Small World" begins (OCR 2008, track 22, 3'16"). The girls' vocal presence in this counterpoint undermines Rose's calculating nature in "Small World," allowing the audience to hear a musically opposing, alternate perspective of the situation. While the counterpoint sounds fluid from a musical viewpoint, it does not work successfully in performance because it also comes across as conflicting; the audience struggles to listen to one duet over the other as the two pairs sing over each other. At one point, the two girls sing in harmonic thirds over Herbie's solo moment, and Rose can be heard making a "shhhh" sound at them (OCR 2008, track 22, 3'48"). This comic mother–daughter opposition draws attention away from Herbie but also exposes Rose's scheme; the girls are commenting on her tactics and she does not want Herbie to become aware of their presence – or of what they know.

This number complicates the perception of Rose's madness; its removal from the show does not necessarily make her character more or less mad, but rather omits certain aspects of her madness that would have made for a more complex personality. The lyrics of the song are best summarized in the last stanza of the section that precedes the counterpoint with "Small World," in which the girls sing that "when Momma's done not a soul survives" and "Everybody run for your lives." The comically terrifying image conjured by the final two lines depicts Rose as dangerous – a step beyond manipulative and clever, even if the girls are speaking in hyperbole. Since this number's removal equates to the omission of that frightening side of Rose's character, her predatory nature is kept in check. Overall, however, the argument can also be made that perhaps it is best that Rose does not come across as quite so monstrous, for even an anti-hero must remain somewhat likeable if the audience is to remain invested in her. This number's perspective on Rose's villainy would have elevated the audience's perception of her madness – perhaps too much, at such an early moment in the show. On the other hand, inclusion of "Momma's Talkin' Soft" in the show would have added depth to "Rose's Turn"; the use of this number in the mad scene serves as reference to Rose's more treacherous side that is completely lost because of the cut, perhaps to the scene's detriment.

"If Momma Was Married"

Louise and June's duet "If Momma Was Married" occurs in Act I scene 9 and is set in the office of theater manager Mr. Grantzinger, who is considering June and the act for his theater. In the scene, a disgruntled June fantasizes about a "normal" mother and life away from the stage. She exclaims, "Momma can do one thing: she can make herself believe anything she makes up … she even believes the act is good." June claims to hate the act, and when Louise argues that "you can't blame everything on Momma," June counters: "*You* can't maybe. I wish she'd marry Herbie and let me alone" (Laurents, 1989: 47). While Louise does not agree that Herbie, whom she naively thinks is too interested in show business himself to be romantically inclined toward Rose, would be the man for Momma, she does concur that Momma should marry and adopt a more socially acceptable role as housewife. The girls imagine a domestic, simple life away from Rose's delusions, her unstoppable ambition, and her adherence to nontraditional gender roles.

The number might as well be titled "If Momma Was Normal," or "If Momma Was a Socially Acceptable Woman." June's and Louise's desire for a domestic life reflects the expectations of society and the typical Broadway musical itself; Rose's lack thereof breaks conventions of the genre, as discussed in previous sections of this Element. The sisters' desire for a sense of "normalcy" in their lives portrays the complexity inherent to Rose's choices and the fact that her social nonconformity is not a black-and-white issue. For, although June and Louise sing together about the same subject, their own motivations are quite opposite; their combined views reveal two of Rose's major character traits.

Louise wants to support Momma in what she thinks will be a happier, simpler life; June wants to marry her off and escape Rose's suffocating involvement in her life.

The number holds some humor that showcases the daughters' perspectives, reflecting such an untraditional upbringing under Rose's care that they do not even know what "normal" really is. For example, Stacy Wolf notes the song's opening lyrics in which Louise imagines a comical vision of a "normal" home life: "If Momma was married we'd live in a house/ As private as private can be/ Just Momma, three ducks, five canaries, a mouse/ Two monkeys, one father, six turtles, and me." Wolf explains, "So unimaginable is a father to June and Louise that they fantasize about him as an addition to their menagerie, no different than another pet" (Wolf, 2002: 118). While this humorous line may just be a gag, it nonetheless portrays the girls' non-normative experience with fatherly relationships.

The musical style of "If Momma was Married" is that of a conventional waltz, and the number's buoyant dance rhythm lends itself to the young sisters' active imaginings in the lyrics (OCR 1959, track 10). Louise and June alternate stanzas, singing in a convivial sequence, or often in unison or pleasant thirds harmony, showcasing a rare moment of tuneful friendliness between the sisters that portrays Rose as an Other – one of daughters versus mother – and that foreshadows her strained relationships with both girls later in the show.

The middle section of "If Momma was Married" borrows from *Gypsy*'s most prominent waltz number, "Let Me Entertain You," moving seamlessly between the original number and the cleverly inserted quotation (OCR 1959, track 10, 1'33"). The two sisters singing this quotation foreshadows the double purpose of the "Let Me Entertain You" number – first used in its original waltz form by Baby June, and later turned into a bluesy-style strip tease by Louise when she becomes "Gypsy Rose Lee." "Momma" Rose's influence is undeniably present in both girls' iterations of the number, and the use of this quotation in "If Momma was Married" suggests that their far-fetched dream – for Rose to marry and for them to live a life away from show business – will never occur.

Although this number is, on the surface, comedic, and underneath, almost sinister – as June and Louise toss their harsh criticism on Rose – it is also extremely revelatory about Rose's refusal to adhere to the norms of domesticity. As an anti-hero, her methods of disrupting these norms are far from perfect – as her disgruntled daughters prove. These over-the-top methods also exemplify her excess – and therefore, to some degree, her madness, as well.

Rose's Turning Point Song: "Everything's Coming Up Roses"

The Act I finale, "Everything's Coming Up Roses," is sung by Rose alone, but unlike the final number "Rose's Turn," this number is not sung to an empty room. As Herbie and Louise stand as spectators to Rose's delusions, gaping at her from the sidelines, they steer the audience into viewing her from their perspectives. As they watch her silently, this number proves that Rose fills enough musical and physical space by herself to satisfy the audience's need for a rousing end to the first Act. This number, along with Rose's preceding monologue, represents a major turning point in the musical's plot. In the scene leading up to the number, Rose finds out that June has secretly eloped with Tulsa and abandoned her family and the troupe to explore a career without them. Unwilling to accept defeat at the loss of her more talented daughter – the troupe's long-standing star – Rose plugs Louise as June's replacement in a fit of desperation.

As Rose initially learns of June's abandonment, she stands "not moving, looking like a dead woman" as Herbie and Louise attempt to convince her to give up the failing act, get married, and start a "normal" life. As they rationalize living a show business-free lifestyle, Rose acts "as though in a trance" while her mind races, completely ignoring their reasonable suggestions (Laurents, 1989: 57–58). Rose responds in an alarming fashion, shifting from deadpan shock to extreme enthusiasm as she locks on to her new idea, "carried away now by her own determination and emotion that she does not see the look that has come over Louise's face" (Laurents, 1959: 1–11–70). As she prepares to burst into emotion-packed song, the stunned responses of Herbie and Louise alert the audience that Rose's state of mind is not grounded in reality.

Rose's monologue preceding the musical number resembles a manic tirade, brought on by her fear of abandonment and fueled by her unquenchable need for success and refusal to be victimized. Rose lists the people who have abandoned her in life – her former husbands, her own mother, and now June – and firmly states, "Well, this time, I'm not crying." As Rose's excessive emotion begins to peek through her hard shell, she is depicted as strong yet also pitiable in her delusions. As the stage directions state that Rose is "now going over the edge," she cries, "[June] is nothing without me! I'm her mother and I made her!" For a moment, Rose's anger appears almost justifiable. Her pivot, however, toward her "untalented" daughter Louise, exposes Rose's unraveling mind. Rose exclaims, trying to convince Herbie, Louise, and herself – described in the stage directions as "an express train out of control" – that Louise "is going to be beautiful! She *is* beautiful! Finished?! We're just beginning and there's no stopping us this time!" (Laurents, 1989: 58–59).

Rose's refusal to accept a more rational plan in favor of her own delusional dreams spirals out of control as she begins to sing, prompted with the stage direction: "Her face alive with fight and plans and happiness, she roars into a violently joyous song about how great everything is going to be" (Laurents, 1959: 1–11–70). The phrase "violently joyous" sums up Rose's erratic behavior; as Arthur Laurents explains,

> At first, Rose is stunned and bewildered; then shock turns to anger and simmers to a boil as she speaks until she is ready to kill. Kill she does, and as she does, her need for revenge right now, this minute, shatters all sense. She goes around the bend and we have a temporarily crazy woman singing and believing "Everything's Coming Up Roses." (Laurents, 2009: 80)

The number begins with the "I had a dream" motive (OCR 1959, track 12, 0'03"), recognizable here from its earlier appearance in "Some People" and foreshadowing the motive's later importance in "Rose's Turn." This motive serves as a signifier of her madness when it occurs in the score. In "Everything's Coming Up Roses," the "I had a dream" motive's single iteration at the very beginning rings like a warning bell.

Beneath Rose's singing in the first ten measures lies an ominous tremolo in the timpani and cello. This oscillating dominant B-flat within an E-flat major sonority creates a sense of anticipation and excitement, holding the audience to the edge of their seats while they wait to hear what Rose's "dream" is all about. Then, in measure 11, a chromatic modulation brings the song into the key of B major, shifting in tandem with Rose's burst of determination: "You'll be swell! You'll be great!" (OCR 1959, track 12, 0'21"). This pivotal moment is ripe for analysis of Rose as a "temporarily crazy woman," as Laurents describes.

The primary example of this assessment within the music of "Everything's Coming Up Roses" lies in the constant use of repetition. In this number, Styne's use of repetitive musical phrases demonstrates how Rose fits into this operatic madwoman mold. For example, the titular phrase "everything's coming up roses" occurs at the end of every section. Additionally, the final verse of "Everything's Coming Up Roses" particularly emphasizes Rose's sudden show of excess with its repetitious, erratic, and fantastic language. Rose repeats the titular line again and again, with outrageous statements of optimism about what is in store. She exclaims how everything's coming up "roses and daffodils," "sunshine and Santa Claus," "bright lights and lollipops." Excessive repetition of the same irrational idea – fairytale-like success – signals Rose's separation from reality, as if she is not merely trying to convince her onlookers but also herself.

Not only is the maddened repetition present in the lyrics, but also in the music. Each of the repeated lyric lines features the exact same melodic pattern:

oscillation between G-sharp and F-sharp in a jarring mixed meter, only changing in dynamics as each line gradually crescendos (OCR 1959, track 12, 2'28"). In Rose's final iteration of the titular phrase, she adds: "Everything's coming up roses *for me and for you.*" Hidden in the words "for me," Rose's true motivation is exposed. These two small, foreshadowing words return in a much less subtle revelation at the end of "Rose's Turn," when they are repeated five times in a fitful finale, after Louise does finally have success and Rose still finds herself wanting – and, in the context of that scene, fully mad.

4 "Rose's Turn": Analyzing *Gypsy*'s Mad Scene

"Rose's Turn" is *Gypsy*'s climax number and Rose's true mad scene. As Rose has been observed before this scene as being overly dramatic, deceitful, and power-driven, the argument could be made that "Rose's Turn" is merely a soliloquy of the innermost thoughts and desires of a larger-than-life and self-centered character. So, what makes this number a mad scene? Three main elements contribute to this designation: the scene's positioning as the climax within the arc of the plot, the use of operatic compositional techniques in the music that traditionally portray madness, and the performative elements of madness displayed in the various iterations over the years by the actors who have played Rose on stage and film. My theoretical move in this section is not to reclaim or redefine this description, but rather to provide a full analysis of Rose's mad scene in both a feminist and a musical framework.

"Rose's Turn" as an Operatic Mad Scene

"Rose's Turn" is frequently described by analysts as an "aria" or with similar operatic terminology. Sondheim recalls that Ethel Merman herself described it as "sorta more an aria than a song," as she strove to understand and capture the number's grandness (Sondheim, 2011: 77). "Rose's Turn" elevates *Gypsy* into the operatic realm; Ethan Mordden, for example, argues that "in 'Rose's Turn,' many themes collide – the star stuff, the story stuff, the director-choreographer stuff, the musical-behaving-with-opera's-power stuff" (Mordden, 1998: 250).

Analysis of "Rose's Turn" as an operatic mad scene begs the questions: does Rose's madness empower or weaken her? And does her madness control her, or does she maintain her agency of self? Ultimately, the audience witnesses a woman empowered through the number's music, yet simultaneously weakened by the narcissism exposed in the lyrics and the mental fragmentation it causes.

Musically, "Rose's Turn" comprises "fragments of all the songs associated with [Rose] and the people in her life: the songs we've heard all evening, colliding in an extended surreal medley consisting of fragments of the score," as Stephen Sondheim explains (Sondheim, 2011: 77). The series of fragments in "Rose's Turn" allows for Rose to reinterpret her actions that have occurred throughout the show while, from a musical standpoint, also exhibiting an impressive display of vocal talent through the belting style, made famous by Ethel Merman. The number's musical style, though clearly fashioned using the methods of a musical play, in some ways likens Rose's mad scene to Lucia di Lammermoor's operatic one. As Susan McClary explains that "in the Mad Scene, [Lucia] finally abandons formal convention altogether to enact a collaged fantasia (McClary, 1991: loc. 1351). Rose, while not displaying the extreme violence of the operatic Lucia that leads to a complete abandonment of formal convention, similarly breaks free from the confines of musical style to perform her own fragmented mad scene or "collaged fantasia" in "Rose's Turn."

Another relevant comparison of the two mad scenes involves their respective audiences. While both Lucia and Rose enact their scenes for the "real" audience – the theatergoers – Lucia's scene also features an on-stage audience of other characters, whereas Rose performs only for herself. The audience of any female character's mad scene creates a complicated framework of analysis, for it produces both a gendered and a psychological "gaze." The concept of the specific "male gaze," originally coined by feminist film theorist Laura Mulvey, refers to the common occurrence of an active, engaged male subject and passive, submissive female object within Western patriarchal society (Mulvey, 1975). Other feminist scholars since, however, have expanded upon and complicated this concept; Stacy Wolf, for example, argues the existence of a "female" or "lesbian" gaze in the musical *Gypsy* (Wolf, 2002: 109). Hannah Dickson's thesis "Performing Agency – Contemporary Burlesque and the Feminist Gaze" (2002) provides ample theoretical analysis of the "feminist" gaze within burlesque specifically; this analysis relates particularly well to Rose's strip sequence in "Rose's Turn."

"Rose's Turn" Overview

Within *Gypsy*'s plot, "Rose's Turn" is the "eleven o'clock" number, occurring right before the final scene of the play. Rose becomes galvanized to sing "Rose's Turn" after a disturbing argument with Louise (or rather, at this point in the story, Gypsy Rose Lee) that makes Rose reflect on her current state of unhappiness and lack of purpose within Louise's new career. In the scene prior to "Rose's Turn," Rose asks her daughter, "What'd I do it for? You say I fought my whole life. I fought *your* whole life. So now tell me: *what'd I do it for?*" and Louise replies, after a long pause, "I thought you did it for me, Momma" (Laurents, 1989: 103). Rose exits Louise's dressing room and enters the empty burlesque stage, alone with her thoughts. As the mad scene begins,

Rose stands alone on stage in a single spotlight. Her scene starts with a monologue that melds into the vocal number, transitioning into music after the shouted declaration:

> You wanna know what I did it for?! *Because I was born too soon and started too late, that's why!* With what I have in me, I could've been better than ANY OF YOU! What I got in me – what I been holding down inside of me – if I ever let it out, there wouldn't be signs big enough! There wouldn't be lights bright enough! HERE SHE IS, BOYS! HERE SHE IS, WORLD! HERE'S ROSE!! (Laurents, 1989: 104)

The monologue reveals what much of "Rose's Turn" is about: a woman who realizes her life as she knows it is over because (1) both of her children have now either abandoned her or lost their need for her, and (2) she herself "was born too soon and started too late" for her own success, yet she refuses to surrender to that reality. In one final push to prove herself, she performs "Rose's Turn" to showcase her unrealized "talents" to herself, to the people she has lost (Herbie, June, and Louise), and to the imaginary "world." Moreover, she shows how she truly wants – and has always wanted – to be a star herself, rather than promote the success of her children. This number stands as Rose's only moment in *Gypsy* to "be a star," revealing what she may have been like on stage as a performer had she ever succeeded. The psychological state Rose displays throughout the song is the result of her realization of this failure, coupled with newfound loneliness as a mother.

From a formal standpoint, "Rose's Turn" follows musical structure evocative of the operatic arias of the nineteenth-century Italian bel canto style. The two-tempo aria structure, also known as "la solita forma," exemplified in works by Rossini, Bellini, Verdi, and the like, is shown in Table 2.

Harold S. Powers refers to each section as either "kinetic," moving the aria forward, or "static," focusing on a character's internal thought (Powers, 1987: 69). While "Rose's Turn" does not follow this form exactly, it contains several similarities that render it reminiscent of "la solita forma" style.

The musical structure of "Rose's Turn" is comprised of two larger parts, here labeled A and B, each with their own smaller ab structure. Part A includes the exposition, similar to the kinetic "tempo d'attacco" of an aria, and a section in which Rose imagines herself a stripper, the static "cantabile" section. The end of Part A and beginning of Part B serve as a turning point, a kinetic "tempo di mezzo," in which Rose begins to see the gravity of reality. Then she surrenders to the imaginings of Part A, letting the delusions take over as she finishes the number in a rousing yet static "cabaletta." A full outline of this interpretation of the musical structure is provided in Table 3.

Table 2 Two-tempo aria structure

Scena/recitative (followed by) Tempo d'attacco (kinetic)	Cantabile (lyrical, expository) (static)	Tempo di Mezzo (kinetic)	Cabaletta (rousing, often followed by coda) (static)

Table 3 Formal analysis of "Rose's Turn"

Section	Measures/time stamp	Lyrical themes	Musical themes
A: a	mm. 1–45 (OCR 1959, track 16, beginning –1'42")	- Speaking parts - Striptease	- "Let me entertain you" brass triplets (borrowed from "Gypsy Strip Routine") - "Some People" theme
A: b	mm. 46–62 (OCR 1959, track 16, 1'42"–2'16")	- The series of statements ("Momma's ____"), two voices in her head speaking to each other (going mad) - Lyric quotation from cut number "Momma's Talkin' Soft"	- Ostinato chords - Highly repetitive melody
B: a	mm. 63–127 (OCR 1959, track 16, 2'16"–3'35")	- Rant with ostinato - "I had a dream"	- Ostinato played, then sung and played, then sung - "I had a dream" motive
B: b	mm. 128–145 (OCR 1959, track 16, 3'35"–4'26")	- "everything's coming up roses" - "for me"	- Quote of "Everything's Coming Up Roses" mixed with triplets motif from A section

A Section, part a (mm. 1–45)

Musically, the opening section of "Rose's Turn" reflects Rose's own erratic and spiraling thoughts, quoting multiple motives and parts of numbers from throughout the show. It opens with brassy triplets reminiscent of the previous song, "Gypsy's Strip Routine (Let Me Entertain You)" from Act II scene 5. Rose's first lyrics, "Curtain up! Light the lights!" set the stage for her spotlight number, while showcasing the same musical phrase used in "Everything's Coming Up Roses" in a different key and with a more hurried and desperate rhythm (OCR 1959, track 16, 0'07"). This borrowed phrase adds to Rose's jealous tone as she envies Louise's success – a success for which the seed was planted with that Act I finale – that hangs over this entire number.

Rose interacts with an imaginary audience of "boys" as she begins her improvised striptease, exclaiming twice that she's "got it" as the brass section's flutters and slides urge her on. As she asks, "You like it?" the "boys" of the live pit orchestra enthusiastically reply, "Yeah!" (OCR 1959, track 16, 0'36"). This opening section serves as Rose's only interaction with other "people" during the number, a brief breaking of the fourth wall as the orchestra members get their own spoken line, reinforcing the fact that the song and strip exist only in Rose's head. The swinging brass instrumentation in this section is associated with the typical style used in burlesque music, and perhaps also represents Rose's own "brassy" personality. It also serves another purpose in this number; the function of the brass instruments in Rose's head is not unlike that of the flute in Lucia's mad scene, which represents her hallucinations.[7]

Rose appears similarly sated by her performance in this part of the number, encouraged by the orchestra and powerful, jazzy style of the music in this section. After Rose starts the number by teasing the "boys," she enters into a quotation of "Some People," except this version features a swing rhythm, and the lyrics: "Some people got it and make it pay/ Some people can't even give it away!/ This people's got it/ And this people's spreadin' it around./ You either have it,/ Or you've had it" (OCR 1959, track 16, 0'44"). After each of the last three lines, the accompanying orchestral striptease triplet pattern repeats, encouraging Rose on her imaginary stage. The final lines, "You either have it, or you've had it," reflect Rose's continual insistence that she's "got it," while simultaneously allowing the audience to infer that she is, actually, past her prime and entering a state of disillusionment, anger, and delusion.

---

[7] The use of the flute to represent madness is not unique to *Lucia di Lammermoor*. It can also be found in Bellini's *Norma* and *La sonnambula* and Strauss's *Salome*, among others.

The striptease continues for several bars while the orchestra repeats the triplet motif and Rose mockingly attempts to seduce the audience. She echoes lines from earlier in the show, turning them into sexy hooks – but the act does not particularly work, rather creating an uncanny regurgitation of Rose's memories in an incongruous, sexualized fashion. She first declares, "Hello everybody! My name is Rose. What's yours?" in an imitation of Baby June from the child's vaudeville performances as well as of Louise in her strip act. Often performed in a mocking "baby" voice, this line may come off as humorous or uncomfortable, but not sexy. Rose then shouts, "How d'ya like them egg rolls, Mister Goldstone?" while clearly indicating that the "egg rolls" refer to her breasts. Though enacted with varying degrees of sexual excess by different performers over the years on film and stage, in no performance does Rose actually "strip" out of any clothes besides perhaps a coat or scarf, so the illusion of the striptease act remains in her head. In all performances, however, the dual purpose behind Rose's sexual display in this opening section is clear: she is jealously imitating Louise's "Gypsy Rose Lee" persona, and she is delusional, performing an act to an imaginary audience. As she sings her final line of this section, "Hold your hats and hallelujah, Momma's gonna show it to ya," Rose launches into a silent striptease accompanied by the swinging orchestra for six bars (OCR 1959, track 16, 1'27").

In this strip section, we hear excessive musical repetition – the first of several appearances of this compositional technique in the number. Although apparent to a larger degree in the B section, Styne uses repetition here through the constant reiteration of the two-measure brassy triplet motif from the number's opening (OCR 1959, track 16, 0'9").

Rose's silent strip occurs at the very end of this section, and the music of this six-measure interlude jars the audience with a level of dissonance heretofore unheard in this number (OCR 1959, track 16, 1'29"), displaying a moment of chromatic excess. In an interview with Michael Feinstein (2009), Styne explains his compositional goals in this passage:

Styne: I even put Prokofiev in there, but nobody noticed it, for four bars.[8] You know with the trumpet solo, in between [syllabic singing of the melody].

Feinstein: Yes, in "Rose's Turn," yes.

Styne: I put it in there because I tried to find this woman who is somebody who, well, she's going crazy out there, you know what I'm saying? Blaming the whole world, [incoherent], well, finally she's doing everything for herself. The guilt – exposition of the soliloquy – so, the music had to do a lot of explaining, a lot of *feeling*.

---

[8]　As earlier stated, it is actually six bars.

Although Styne does not specify which composition of Prokofiev he quotes in this discordant passage, the effect of including this passage reminiscent of the Russian composer's occasionally dissonant style in the score is clear. As this jarring section resembles twentieth-century Neoclassicism much more closely than the rest of this number – or the rest of the *Gypsy* score, for that matter – it represents how Rose's mental state in this moment is also dissonant, discordant with the rest of the "sane" characters in the show, and unraveling away from the "normal" world of tonality.

Rose's overt display of sexuality in this section creates fertile ground for feminist theoretical analysis. Within the context of the show, the striptease appears shocking to witness from the middle-aged Rose who, at this stage in her life, is not a performer, much less a burlesque performer who strips. Moreover, it is shocking because it feels out of character for the Rose that the audience has witnessed up to this point in the show. Although not known for clean moral judgment, Rose has made it clear that she possesses little admiration for burlesque or any of the stripping acts that it entails. This is partially because, as she says in Act II scene 2, "when a vaudeville act plays in burlesque, that means it's all washed up" (Laurents, 1989: 77). Of course, in Act II scene 4, she changes her stance, exclaiming to Louise, " . . . we can walk away proud because we made it! Maybe only in burlesque, maybe only in second-rate burlesque at that – but let's walk away a star!" (Laurents, 1989: 90). But even still, Rose insists on Louise being "pure" without any of the "vulgar junk" that other strippers wear, maintaining a false sense of morality regarding women's sexualized, bodily display.

This section of "Rose's Turn" reveals a madness linked to the portrayal of sexual excess, as discussed by opera scholars such as Susan McClary, who argues that this association illuminates the problematic nature of demonizing women who "should not" possess sexuality because their non-normative version of it is seen as abject. Up to this point in the show, the audience has never witnessed explicit sexuality from Rose. Thus, this excessively sensual performance is both surprising and could, on the surface, be seen as "abject." Not unlike her operatic predecessors such as Richard Strauss's Salome, whose violent depiction of sexuality forces it into the world of the abject, or George Bizet's Carmen, whose freedom of sexual expression results in her demise, Rose's sexual display in this number may be interpreted as abject for two reasons: (1) she is "old," an aging mother figure, and (2) her purpose in this number is not to entertain, but rather she is self-performing sexuality for an imaginary audience – an act perhaps better left behind closed doors. Both reasons set her apart from her daughter, Gypsy, and also from the strippers who sing "You Gotta Have a Gimmick," for example, who, though older and less conventionally beautiful than the typical successful burlesque performer, use their sexuality for humor and entertainment and are therefore viewed as displaying "acceptable" sexual expression for *Gypsy*'s audience. However, Rose's strip may also be interpreted as being empowered, revealing Rose's agency to reclaim these "abject" acts as her own.

The lack of an on-stage audience in "Rose's Turn" also complicates our interpretation of the number as a mad scene and Rose's level of agency within the strip section specifically. Lucia di Lammermoor's mad scene, for example, is simultaneously in her head and out in the open; she exists in such a state of madness that she is unaware of her voyeurs, but the aghast reactions of the other characters reinforce the "real" audience's understanding of the scene as clearly being a mad scene. "Rose's Turn," on the other hand, feels more like an intrusion into a private moment, in which Rose performs the strip for her own pleasure. As the entire scene is in Rose's head, the audience is left to interpret her delusional actions on their own. Arthur Laurents explains:

> Louise's strip is topped by another strip, this one by a desperate, crazed middle-aged woman who doesn't actually strip because it's all taking place in the only place she *could* strip: in her recognition-hungry head. It's Rose's turn in the limelight, and high time, too. In her head, she is the greatest striptease queen in the world; in her head, she can bring down the house; in her head, she is the star of stars and can take all those bows. (Laurents, 2009: 34)

In many ways, Rose's audience transcends gender and creates a nuanced "gaze." Her audience is in her head; the "real" audience watching *Gypsy* simply spectates from outside this imaginary stage. Rose does declare "Here she is, boys!" implying that she, like her daughter in burlesque, performs her strip for a male audience, but the mad nature of this number denies the voyeur his typical gaze. Although catering to the "boys," Rose is far from being the passive object of the patriarchal "male gaze"; galvanized by her madness, she gains the agency required to become an active object. Refusing to be a passive or submissive object, Rose engages the "feminist gaze"; not catering to men or women, she acts in a way that, according to Hannah Dickson's theory, exists as an

> active refusal and disentanglement of the male gaze … [that] allow[s] the performer to reject this way of being seen by others and find their own empowerment and agency through a performance of their sexuality that is done for themselves, to resist oppression and celebrate their own pleasure. (Dickson, 2022: 1)

As previously discussed, Rose's strip – the attempt of a middle-aged woman to imitate her daughter – might, on one hand, be seen as grotesque from some members of the audience. On the other hand, it may be interpreted as a display of sensual prowess. Discussing Ethel Merman's performance specifically, Stacy Wolf argues that "descriptions of Rose suggest that … her power and forcefulness called up wonder and awe but neither identifications of desire ("I want her") nor identifications of admiration ("I want to be like her") (Wolf, 2002: 109). If anything, Rose's strip elicits feelings of pity. Ultimately, however, the audience's interpretation of Rose's sexual display does not matter, because Rose, gaining agency through her madness, eludes the voyeur in favor of a self-indulgent, feminist gaze. At the end of Rose's turn, we also become privy to Rose's secret audience of one – Louise, clapping from the sidelines, walks onto stage at the number's end. While we do not know how much of the number she has witnessed, Louise's presence creates a female solidarity on stage and reinforces the feminist gaze.

A Section, part b (mm. 46–62)

The A section takes a turn in measure 46, when the Prokofiev-inspired passage abruptly ends and Rose suddenly speaks over a silent orchestra, "Ready or not (shh), Here comes Momma!" and then the orchestra enters into a rapid key change and overall shift in mood (OCR 1959, track 16, 1'38"). This part becomes almost monotonously repetitive as Rose sings the same musical phrase for each line of lyrics over a simple boom-chick accompaniment. The lyrics of this part are borrowed from the cut number "Momma's Talkin' Soft."

Rose refers to herself as "Momma" throughout the lyrics in this segment, but the actions "Momma" takes in each line oscillate between two different voices in her head: the confident, strong Momma who's "got it," indicated by lines such as "Momma's talkin' loud,/ Momma's doin' fine,/ Momma's gettin' hot,/ Momma's goin' strong," and the washed-up, mentally unstable Momma who's "gotta let go," as heard in lines like "Momma's movin' on,/ Momma's all alone" and "Momma's gotta move,/ Momma's gotta go." Toward the end of this rant, Rose falters repeatedly, realizing the underlying meaning of the words she sings as she unwittingly declares that "Momma's lettin' go" and "Momma's gotta let go." She begins to realize that her very identity – up to this point, always related to the success of her daughters – is at risk, because June is long gone and Louise is independently famous and no longer needs Rose's help with her career. The first time Rose stumbles here, repeating "Momma" in spoken, arrhythmic bursts as if to clarify the meaning of the word in her head, or simply not knowing how to continue from this jarring moment of realization, one thing becomes clear: the spell of her striptease and faux self-assurance from earlier in the number is broken (OCR 1959, track 16, 1'59"). She is suddenly vulnerable and beaten in the middle of her big show-stopper, and the pretense of Rose's confidence shatters under the reality of her madness and despair.

In a review of *Gypsy* at the Engeman Theater in Northport, New York, journalist Barbara Shuler writes that "when, at the end, Mama takes the stage for the heartbreaking 'Rose's Turn,' you finally understand her years of torment, of trying to live through her children. 'Mama's lettin' go,' she sings. But, truthfully, you don't believe that for a minute" (Schuler, 2017). Rose refuses to believe it, either. Although this part ushers in the B Section by revealing her inner turmoil, it also opens the doors of Rose's true descent into madness: her stark refusal to acknowledge the reality that "Momma's gotta let go." The B Section that follows represents Rose's declaration of the imaginary world as she now chooses to see it, but as it will never truly be.

B Section, part a (mm. 63–127)

The second section of "Rose's Turn" has a markedly different feel than the first, reflecting Rose's drastic change in mood. Part a of this section is Rose's revelation: her moment of clarity before the madness fully sets in. This part is recognizable by the famous two-measure ostinato, originally featured in a different key in "Some People." Here, the mesmerizing D-C#-B-G descending pattern appears in the accompaniment throughout and in Rose's own melody (OCR 1959, track 16, 2'16"). The chromaticism in the first interval of the pattern contributes to the notion of excess/madness delineated by McClary, as well as its repetition throughout the number, discussed further next.

The breakdown of this segment follows the changes in the ostinato pattern, as shown in Table 4.

Table 4 "Rose's Turn" ostinato pattern analysis

mm. 63–94	Ostinato continuous in accompaniment; ostinato melody in vocal part with multi-measure breaks
mm. 95–115	Ostinato continuous in accompaniment; "I had a dream" motive in vocal melody
mm. 116–127	Ostinato disappears in accompaniment, single chord every two measures instead; ostinato reappears continuously in vocal part

Regarding the ostinato that defines this section of the number, Jule Styne stated in an interview that Stephen Sondheim originally did not want the ostinato melody used in the vocal part. As with all interviews, it is important to note that Styne's report should be taken with a grain of salt, as the creators' memories tend to differ in such accounts.[9] Styne claims in his interview with Feinstein (2009) that, though he generally respected Sondheim's expertise, "the only one thing [Sondheim] fought me on was the [*hums ostinato melody*]. He said, 'That's an instrumental passage' … I said, 'No, write words to that.'" According to this report, Styne won that argument, and the result was a show-defining musical motive that became the hallmark of Rose's character.

The ostinato's continual appearance throughout this section of the number makes use of the classic compositional technique of repetition designed to show madness. The repetition of this motif is so persistent throughout this passage that it becomes almost maddening to the listener, but it also demonstrates how Rose's own thoughts are refusing to evolve, spiraling around and around in a pool of irrationality. In the first subsection of this part, indicated in Table 4, the orchestra begins the ostinato as if playing the very thoughts within Rose's mind. She then joins in, as if to speak her thoughts aloud. As these thoughts circulate, she begins to ask – and answer – her own questions about her past and current life. Rose sings a conversation with herself: "Why did I do it?/ What did it get me?/ Scrapbooks full of me in the background./ Give 'em love and what does it get you?/ What does it get you?/ One quick look as each of 'em leaves you." In measure 85, at the line "All your life," the bassline accompaniment switches from a pedal chord to a climbing one-measure E-F#-G-B pattern that continually and ominously repeats, adding to the tension and building to the vocal melody change that occurs in the second subsection.

Starting in measure 95, Rose sings a quotation of her now-familiar "I had a dream" motive (OCR 1959, track 16, 2'56"). This subsection serves as a sort of interlude, a unique moment in the number in which Rose names the other characters in her life: "I had a dream./ I dreamed it for you, June./ It wasn't for me, Herbie./ And if it wasn't for me/ Then where would you be,/ Miss Gypsy Rose Lee?" This moment of reminiscence *almost* serves as a turning point where Rose shows signs of selflessness, but by the end of it, when she addresses Louise (notably using her now-successful stage name "Miss Gypsy Rose Lee"

---

9   Sondheim claims that he laid out the entire number of "Rose's Turn" with choreographer Jerome Robbins before Styne was even involved. He says it was already "outlined and ready for detail work" and that, when he then brought it to Styne, they completed it within the day (Sondheim, 2011: 77).

in a mocking tone), her narcissism wins out. Again, Sondheim's clever lyrics use a turn of phrase – the line "it wasn't for me" shifts from a selfless statement when addressing Herbie into a conditional one ("*if* it wasn't for me") that claims Rose's singular position as the cornerstone of Louise's success. The last three lines of this part are often performed as shout-singing, adding to the sense of extreme emotion (OCR 1959, track 16, 3'18").

Hereafter, Rose truly begins to derail into a mad tirade, again singing the ostinato melody, now with minimal orchestral accompaniment. This final sub-section marks the end of Rose's self-reflection as she collapses into the delusional strip-version of herself from the beginning of the number. The transitional lyrics include the opening line that reveal the origin of the number's title "Rose's Turn": "Well, someone tell me when is it my turn?/ Don't I get a dream for myself?/ Startin' now it's gonna be my turn!/ Gangway, world, get offa' my runway!/ Startin' now, I bat a thousand!/ This time, boys, I'm takin' the bows . . . " This section possesses a sense of urgency and desperation that Rose has hitherto only hinted at, but never uttered aloud – an apt precursor to the declamatory final section.

B Section, part b (mm. 128–145)

The final part of the B section appears with an abrupt key change and another shift in mood (OCR 1959, track 16, 3'35"). It begins with a quotation: "And everything's coming up Rose," applying a subtle alteration to the last word as her own name, rather than the "roses" of the Act I finale. She repeats the phrase twice more using the original "roses," as if to correct herself or to solidify the mad notion of positivity of her future, quipping "for me" after the second iteration. She continues to restate the phrase "for me!" a total of five more times. Between each of these phrases, the now-familiar brassy triplet pattern sounds, but each iteration gets progressively shorter; this truncated feeling contributes to the *molto agitato* direction in measure 137 (OCR 1959, track 16, 3'50"). As suggested, the brass represents her madness, and the frenetic, evolving quality of the triplets in this section creates a heightened sense of disorientation.

At that same measure, some performers begin shouting "for me!" rather than singing it, often applying a hurried sense of aggressive desperation to the phrase. Rose repeats the words again and again as if to convince the imaginary audience – or possibly herself – of the fact that this moment, this show, this career, has not been for the benefit of her daughters, but for *her,* and that she deserves the spotlight, even though it exists only in her head. The last "FOR ME!" written in all caps in Laurents's published libretto, and held out for the longest rhythmic value featured thus far in the song, creates a show-stopping finale moment in which Rose belts the word "me" as long as possible while the orchestra encourages her with frenzied slides and tremolos in a feverish ending (OCR 1959, track 16, 4'06").

Overall, the music in the number's last section clearly represents Rose's excess in its frantic nature and repetition, and in the way that it "plays along" to Rose's fantasies. Although this last subsection is quite short, it stands out from the rest of the number because it serves as the pinnacle of the mad scene. In this part, Rose abandons all acknowledgments of the past, of her relationships to others, and even her role as a mother – she markedly never refers to herself as "Momma" here. Instead, she has replaced it with the identity of "Rose": a self-proclaimed star for whom "everything's coming up roses," that is, for whom an imaginary future shines bright. In most productions of *Gypsy*, this section also includes a dramatic staging cue; at the moment when she belts "everything's coming up Rose," her name lights up in large letters behind her.

Arthur Laurents describes that

> the intention underlying the number was to bring Rose to the point where she finally acknowledges she did everything for herself. Acknowledgment doesn't mean change, however; Rose wouldn't change and she doesn't: she goes right back to doing it all for herself all over again. (Laurents, 2000: 394)

Stephen Sondheim also states that Rose

> was that dramatist's dream, the self-deluded protagonist who comes to a tragic/ triumphant end … Self-delusion, moreover, gives the actor a subtext to play that can flavor every moment; actors can only be grateful to have a song in which they sing 'Everything's so white' while sitting in a blue set. Rose is the classroom example of self-delusion, a showbiz Oedipus. (Sondheim, 2011: 56)

This ending, in which Rose claims the opposite of what the audience knows to be rationally true, also serves as the finale number of the entire musical. Although Rose "survives" the mad scene, unlike many of her operatic mad-women predecessors, her life as she knows it – a life equally defined by show business and motherhood – is over. She never does succeed in finding "a dream for herself," as she so desperately claims to want in "Rose's Turn." Rather, Rose's ending is bleak, shrouded in shrinking possibilities and obvious dead-ends. The final scene proves that her own spotlight will never shine, and that her daughter no longer needs her.

Rose bows after "Rose's Turn" only to find that her mad scene had an unseen audience of one: Louise, watching from the sidelines. Rose finally acknow-ledges to Louise, "I guess I did do it for me" because she "just wanted to be noticed." She crumbles into Louise's arms in a brief moment of feebleness, but the moment quickly passes and Rose reinstates her familiar pretense of strong-headedness and mother-knows-best attitude. Louise then invites Rose to a fancy party – clearly out of pity, though Rose does not seem aware of this – and lends her a mink coat, to which Rose says, comically but also fancifully, "this looks better on me than on you! … Funny how we can both wear the same size" (Laurents, 1959: 2–6–57).

This scene – and Rose's character arc in *Gypsy* – ends with a familiar theme: another "dream." She describes a publicity poster featuring herself and Gypsy, "wearing exactly the same gown … and the headline said: Madame Rose – and her daughter, Gypsy!" As Louise – and the audience – react to this preposterous notion with either mockery or sympathy, the subtext is clear: Rose is unable to face reality, and she has irrevocably succumbed to the madness witnessed in "Rose's Turn."

Authoring Madness in "Rose's Turn"

Ethel Merman, as the original Rose, participated in the creation and authorship of the character. Her mannerisms, her personality, and most importantly, her voice – have become iconic, and her involvement in the shaping of Momma Rose on stage was crucial to the development and legacy of that character within productions of *Gypsy*. A comparison of three renditions of "Rose's Turn" – by Ethel Merman, Angela Lansbury, and Imelda Staunton – demonstrates the importance of performer-authorship and the elevation of a character's madness from the paper to the stage.

Ethel Merman's "Rose's Turn"

"Rose's Turn" was the greatest test of Merman's acting chops in *Gypsy*. Although no video recording exists of her performance of "Rose's Turn," evidence such as the original cast recording, numerous newspaper reviews, the creators' memoirs, and the Jeffrey Magee article on the original "Rose's Turn" provide ample information to create a picture of what Merman would have looked and sounded like. Merman herself considered the number more of an "aria" than a typical song, as mentioned previously, possibly implying that the breadth of the piece spanned beyond her usual skillset. But she was up for the challenge and rose to it in a manner unexpected from her past performance history. Sondheim stated that "despite her misgivings, Ethel triumphed. Not only did she perform ['Rose's Turn'] with vigor and passion, the audience was treated to the spectacle of Ethel Merman, the loud, frozen … low comedienne, singing an 'aria'" (Sondheim, 2011: 77).

Aston described her rendition of "Rose's Turn":

> This is a quick mix of aria, stomp, anthem, hymn, recitative, shout, wail, and ... Miss Merman gives it massive meaning. Doing so, she proves in her noisy fashion to be a singularly effective dramatic actress with a roaring and turbulent capacity for communication. (Aston, 1959)

This "mix" that Aston describes embodies the number's intended operatic feel: a multi-section piece that features complex displays of ranging emotions.

Four moments throughout "Rose's Turn" stand out as crucial to Rose's emotional journey toward madness. The first is the beginning, the A Section "strip." Here, Rose attempts to imitate Louise's "sexiness" in various strip-teases. This section is important within the arc of Rose's mental deterioration in the number because it demonstrates her jealousy of her children, her sudden identity crisis, and her departure from the typical Rose-style vulgarity into a newly forthright display of sexuality.

Unfortunately, this section is also the most difficult to analyze within Ethel Merman's performance of the song because of the nonexistence of a visual recording and the importance of gestures within the strip. Although the lyrics call for certain references to sexuality and her body – her "eggrolls," for instance – Merman's voice in the audio recording does not indicate an embrace of obvious sensuality. Rather, her voice is brash, loud, sometimes gruff, and sounds angry rather than provocative, except for a single moment when she suggestively asks the "boys" of the orchestra, "You like it?" However, as soon as they reply "Yeah!" she retorts with a startling and indignant "Well, I've got it!" (OCR, track 16, 0'40").

A review by critic Brooks Atkinson provides some possible insight into Merman's performance during the number, making no mention of any kind of clear sexual display:

> It is difficult to feel censorious about any character that Miss Merman absorbs into her unique blend of heartiness and drum-major singing ... Her final number, a song written with dramatic versatility by Jule Styne, is a triumph for the character, the actress and the show. The curtain descends on Miss Merman's most dazzling moment ... it is impossible to think about her in any terms except in her own – a supremely self-confident woman with an oval face, popping eyes, a determined mouth, an alert manner of walking and standing, a sure sense of timing and a razzle-dazzle voice. She is not afraid of vulgarity ... When the libretto begins to be affected in the final scenes, she brings it down to earth with a bang. (Atkinson, 1959)

Atkinson's description of Merman as "determined" and "alert" does not necessarily conjure images of a sensual performance, but his observation that "she is not afraid of vulgarity" allows for the possibility of a Merman who fully embraced the striptease in this number. However, Rose's "vulgarity" could represent a number of vices; throughout the show, she is shown to possess no moral compass regarding issues such as theft, manipulation, or lying. In "Rose's Turn," this "vulgarity" could easily refer to her spite, anger, or brashness.

Three other important moments in the number highlight Merman's authorship of the character and her madness. At the end of the A section, Rose falters on the word "Momma" – the part of the number that, according to Sondheim, is the "moment of Rose's breakdown" (OCR, track 16, 1'59"). Sondheim recalls that Merman struggled with the improvisatory nature of the faltering syllables over the accompanying vamp in the orchestra; she focused more on the timing rather than making the words feel natural. He provides a long anecdote that describes her difficulty, explaining that "she wanted to know whether the third syllable (M-M-*M*omma) should be on the downbeat or the upbeat. I explained to her . . . that it didn't matter where the beat was, that the stammer was a sort of mental seizure arising from the line which preceded it" (Sondheim, 2011: 77).

Sondheim further explains that he and Styne "had devised a 'safety bar' – a bar that an orchestra can repeat until the singer is ready to resume singing – so that from night to night she could stammer any way she liked: murmured, explosive, sluggish, hysterical." This assurance was not, apparently, enough for Merman; he recalls that she "concentrated mightily for a moment" and ultimately just asked again, "' . . . but does it come in on the downbeat or the upbeat?'" (Sondheim, 2011: 77).

Arthur Laurents similarly recalls Merman trying and failing to "act" successfully during this part of the number. He notes how well she generally worked with *Gypsy*'s director Jerome Robbins, but how even Robbins could not direct her to perform this particular section with any kind of believability. Although Merman worked with relative success with Robbins's assistant director, Gerald Freedman, Laurents explains:

> Jerry and Ethel had a good rapport; they liked one another and she trusted him. She had a natural flair for lusty comedy but when "Rose's Turn" became dramatic, they were both in trouble. Jerry worked hard and pulled as much out of her as anyone could. Basically, however, she was not an actress and he was unable to help her shift gears when the number reached the stuttering "M-M-M-Momma. (Laurents, 2000: 393)

The next section that reveals a step toward Rose's mental decline is the second half of the B Section, in which the music from "Everything's Coming Up Roses" returns and Rose's mood switches from anger to determination, albeit delusional. In this part, Merman's voice becomes markedly different, changing from her typical belting style to a raspier quality that sounds less supported and more frantic (OCR, track 16, 3'37"). However, she wholly embraces the "for me" repetitions with the strongest belt she can muster, shouting the penultimate few but otherwise giving them the full Merman treatment: a big, rousing finish that, as Sondheim states, "didn't suit the character's meltdown," but does encapsulate the rage that Rose feels in this moment (Sondheim, 2011: 77).

The number's closing became a contested issue among *Gypsy*'s male creators – one which would not be "solved" until the first Broadway revival with Angela Lansbury fifteen years later. Both Sondheim and Laurents describe the controversy in their memoirs. In the final version of the Broadway production, the grandiose final notes of "Rose's Turn" were met with uproarious applause from Merman's adoring audience; in true form – and much like any famous opera diva – Merman bowed in acknowledgment. As Laurents claims, this effectively meant that "at the end of 'Rose's Turn,' Rose left the stage while Ethel Merman took her bow. Bows. Endless. She brought the house down and the show went out the window" (Laurents, 2009: 33). He explains how the entire number is supposed to be in Rose's head, representing a descent into madness – but the bows demolished the fourth wall and thus destroyed the entire dénouement. However, considering Ethel Merman's status as a major star, the bowing and audience response served as more a suspension of the fourth wall than a demolition of it.

This fourth-wall suspending applause was encouraged by none other than Oscar Hammerstein II himself; as Sondheim recalls, the ending of "Rose's Turn" was quite different until Hammerstein convinced them to "allow Ethel to have her deserved thunderous ovation." The original plan, according to Sondheim, was as follows: "I had persuaded Jule [Styne] to end the number on a high, dissonant chord of eerie violin harmonics: a woman having a nervous breakdown would not wind up on a triumphant tonic chord. In the name of purity, I killed the hand." At this dissonant chord, Louise would enter, clapping solo, effectively denying the audience their applause and Merman her bows. In the end, neither Sondheim not Laurents would get their way; Sondheim "gave up and . . . affixed a big ending and a tonic chord to the song," and the potential for an appropriately unnerving ending to Rose's mad scene was somewhat overtaken by the need for Ethel Merman to have a star-quality spotlight moment (Sondheim, 2011: 77).

Critic Brooks Atkinson, however, described Merman/Rose as "saving the show," explaining that

> If there is something fundamentally comic about the character of Mrs. Rose,
> who cheats, cajoles and circumvents, it is because we know that the

opposition is doomed, and that in her own way Miss Merman will save not only Gypsy's career but also the show. (Atkinson, 1959)

The various criticisms from Sondheim and Laurents regarding Merman's performance of "Rose's Turn" – and how it did not align with some of their creative intentions – demonstrate the authorial power inherent to a performer. Merman's interpretation of their music and lyrics became the only version that the audience witnessed and that was recorded on the album of the original Broadway production. Although "Rose's Turn" remains a mad scene regardless, Merman's version of *Gypsy*'s ending is somewhat more optimistic than the creators intended, giving way to the star performer. Reviewer John Chapman described how "at the end of 'Gypsy,' Mama is alone, but she is far from beaten; and, as she is played by Miss Merman, she is wonderful" (Chapman, 1959).

Angela Lansbury's "Rose's Turn"

Lansbury's rendition of "Rose's Turn" depicts a new interpretation of Rose's madness. Whereas Merman portrayed Rose as brash, staunch, and perhaps unhinged, Lansbury showed a Rose who, by the end of the number, is truly mad: so overcome by the realization of her circumstances that she becomes completely out of touch with reality.

While the available video footage of Lansbury in "Rose's Turn" only shows the B Section of the piece, the audio recording gives a hint at what her performance of the A Section may have looked like. Her acting embraces Rose's declining mental state; as critic Walter Kerr describes: "We can expect almost any degree of substance … In the terrible manic downbeat – in the pit and in her fist – of Miss Lansbury's final thrust at nonexistent glory, 'Rose's Turn'" (Kerr, 1974).

In the beginning of the number, Lansbury's performance resembles Merman's in some ways; both are loud and project a bitter attitude. However, Lansbury seems to sing entirely without a smile. While Lansbury's version can come across as uninspired or unvaried, it displays a Rose who has truly lost her ability to emote properly, too driven by her rage. Lansbury's angry presentation and her lack of playfulness in the "strip" section is noticeable as well, particularly in the interaction with the "boys" of the orchestra. Merman, though not as sensual as later performers of the role, entices the "boys" with a suggestive "You like it?" as she begins her strip. Lansbury says this same line with a much angrier tone, emphasizing her hostility (OCR, track 14, 0'42"). At no point does she lighten the mood or relax into a playful attitude. For example, when Rose exclaims, "Ready or not (shh), here comes Momma," Lansbury says this line seething with frustration, through her teeth, rather than with delusional diva-ness, like Merman (OCR 1990, track 14, 1'39").

Lansbury's angry "striptease" – in which she does not provide much sensuality, but rather vexation – neglects to include Rose's pathetic, yet comical, mockery of Louise. According to Arthur Laurents's recollections, Lansbury did attempt some strip moves. He explains:

> She had a beautifully cut red dress for the number, but for the preceding scene in Gypsy's dressing room, she herself had bought a ratty gray cardigan in a musty store … to wear over the red dress. That sweater was what she used to propel herself into the strip: she whipped it off, twirled it around, and flung it into the wings. Everything came easily and natural to her, except the down-and-dirty vulgarity … She had to work hard to get that part of Rose. (Laurents, 2009: 35)

Within the strip section, Lansbury's consistently indignant performance portrays a different type of unhinged behavior, absent of Rose's sexuality, but it can come across as recognizable and empathetic rather than abject or mad. However, her attitude in this section does provide a jarring juxtaposition to the end of the number, in which her display of anger switches to one of complete delusion.

In contrast to the clamorous beginning, the sudden stuttering repeat of the word "Momma" at the end of the A Section serves as a moment of obvious mental breakdown and foreshadows the culmination of Rose's madness at the applause. Angela Lansbury achieves with relative success the section that proved so difficult for Ethel Merman, as Lansbury effectively makes the timing of this section sound more improvised than rehearsed. However, Lansbury's stammering still sounds somewhat forced and occurs too suddenly to allow for total believability, and the transition between her angry tone and then, on the repeat of "Momma," a suddenly startled tone, is less successful (OCR 1990, track 14, 2'00"). Between the quiet, almost mumbled "Momma" repetitions, Lansbury reverts to the loud shout-singing heard before. This sharp contrast implies a battle within Rose's mind: that of anger versus fear.

Extant video footage depicts Lansbury's performance of "Rose's Turn" starting at the beginning of the B Section ("I had a dream"). The existence of this recording proves quite useful for analyzing a strange moment in the number when Lansbury again takes a brief respite from her dominant angry mood. As soon as part b of the B Section begins with the lyric "Everything's coming up Rose," Lansbury switches from a fuming stand-and-point style of singing to something very different: a plastered-on smile with mime-like hands waving stiffly back and forth. Her movements appear frantic, desperate, and oddly childlike – perhaps mimicking her once-young daughters and mocking the futility of the vaudeville path she took them on. Her voice in this section remains brash, but suddenly sounds stiff and detached.

She quickly switches to a different gesture on the words "for me," however; here, she repeatedly points to herself sternly and violently with both hands. As the pointing becomes more and more desperate, her vocal style matches this emotion as it turns from singing to yelling – much like Merman's version, except gruffer and even more aggressive. According to Lansbury, this section, in which Rose finally admits whom she "did it for," is the crux of the entire number. Lansbury explains: "Rose is an extraordinary woman, and the thing is she really, really wanted everything for herself … And 'Rose's Turn' is all about that" (Lansbury, in Peikert, 2020).

The most drastic change that director Laurents made in the revival version of "Rose's Turn" was the ending. As previously mentioned, Ethel Merman's bows after the number – a response to the inevitable uproar of audience applause – did not match the initial intention of certain creative team members, who originally preferred that Rose stay in character, rather than spotlighting Merman the performer. In this first revival version, Laurents discovered a way to keep the bows yet also keep the character. He explains:

> Because of Angie's unique talent, I found justification for the bows at the end of "Rose's Turn." I went back to my original premise: The number takes place in an empty theater, the applause is only in Rose's head; at the end, she is bowing to no one. It is the first time that Angie has taken a bow onstage during the entire show so the audience goes wild: applauding, cheering, screaming. Rose, not Angie, keeps bowing, an odd, demented look in her eyes … she bows again and once again, staring at something that isn't there. The applause begins to die down. More lights go out. Rose still bows … the audience stops applauding. But Rose bows again and the moment is hair-raising because the shocked audience realizes that the whole episode was in Rose's head: it has seen a woman momentarily gone mad. (Laurents, 2000: 395)

Laurents implies that this directorial choice was only possible because Lansbury was a better actress than Merman. But the important new element here is the madness that Lansbury portrays in her final moments of the number's fading glory. Laurents wanted a way to show that the entire number was not reality, but rather a mad delusion, and this ending accomplished that goal.

The post-applause bowing stuck as part of subsequent *Gypsy* performances, and its effect on the character's portrayal stuck, too. Rose is experiencing not merely a nervous breakdown in "Rose's Turn" but a complete disassociation from reality, a mental break: a mad scene.

Imelda Staunton's "Rose's Turn"

In Imelda Staunton's rendition of "Rose's Turn," her movements and voice are hard and desperate – not those befitting a would-be performer, as Rose fancies herself to be, but of someone who clearly considers herself celebrity material. Watching her attempt to show off her "talents" elicits both shock and sympathy. As Matt Trueman states of Staunton's Rose, "it's the combination of determination and delusion that ruins her"; her performance in this number proves that Rose is out of touch with reality, but determined enough to run herself into the ground (Trueman, 2015). Leslie Felperin likewise writes, "her hidden performer instincts taped [*sic*] down deep inside … burst forth with a deeply poignant version of 'Rose's Turn' at the end as her sanity finally snaps" (Felperin, 2015).

As Staunton begins the number, she is, as Susannah Clapp describes, "a tiny figure on a huge stage. A big voice, and behind it gigantic shadows. One of the greatest of musical monsters" (Clapp, 2014). In the opening strip section, Staunton is highly expressive in both voice and movements, portraying a complex range of emotions from the start. She begins singing with an expression of anger resembling the performances of Merman and Lansbury, but soon evolves into a spectrum of constantly changing dispositions, giving the impression that her mood is highly unstable and erratic. Her purpose behind the strip is clearly to mock Louise, as she makes exaggerated gestures and adds whiny and snarling affects to her voice (OCR 2015, track 19, 1'14"). Staunton's mock-strip is not highly sexualized; rather, her gestures are stifled and appear uncomfortable. Michael Billington calls this section "grotesque," describing that "Rose's dream of stardom reaches its apogee in the final number when, as the character breaks down, a mink-wrapped Staunton grotesquely mimics the strip-teasing motions of her now celebrated daughter, Gypsy Rose Lee" (Billington, 2015). Staunton also stumbles in and out of confidence during this section; at the end of part a of the A section, she shakingly falters on her imaginary strip and strugglingly shoves off her coat in a moment of desperate frustration. She quickly recovers, but the façade is soon lost again.

As Staunton enacts the repetitive "Momma" segment at the end of the A Section, her dominant, mocking attitude comes to a screeching halt. First, however, she begins by singing the segment in a disturbingly small voice – babyish, even – that she soon alternates with a guttural, emphatic voice (OCR 2015, track 19, 1'50"), all the while continuing to make stripping gestures and taking off imaginary clothes. As she reaches the stumbling moment on the word

"Momma," she does more than stutter; she quivers with fearful, wild eyes. After attempting to recover, her second stumble shows an entirely new interpretation of this essential moment: she does not stammer the word over an orchestral vamp, but rather the music stops completely as she mouths the word "Momma" over and over with barely audible syllables (OCR 2015, track 19, 2'21"). This moment stands out as unusual in the performance history of "Rose's Turn." Staunton's long, silent struggle is painful to watch, as we clearly see a woman not only disturbed but going completely mad with the realization of her new identity loss and that being a "momma" no longer matters.

Once Staunton finally begins singing again, she starts out defeated (OCR 2015, track 19, 2'42"). This moment is almost pathetic, if not for the undercurrent of treachery that she has established within the character, prohibiting the audience from empathizing with this villainous Rose – a sentiment soon fortified by the outrage she progressively exhibits in the subsequent lines. Once she reaches the "everything's coming up Rose" segment, her foremost expression is utter desperation, clinging to her last shreds of entitlement but without any remaining dignity. As she sings "for me," she can barely get the words out; she half-shouts the last several iterations as "for m –," out of breath and overwhelmed with emotion (OCR 2015, track 19, 4'12"). Staunton musters a final large breath to belt out the last two words. Staunton's final, belting declaration "for me!" leaves the audience with a sense of dread, without even a touch of triumph, despite her skilled vocal abilities (OCR 2015, track 19, 4'19"). This looming feeling makes the audience's applause feel ironic and even inappropriate – for, though Staunton's performance was extraordinary, she makes it clear that Rose is left in the dust, with nothing but her madness remaining. She continues her bows long after the applause, and the feeling persists, hanging in the uncomfortably silent air.

Staunton's "Rose's Turn" is a complete operatic mad scene in every sense, most especially because it truly serves as the catalyst for her ultimate demise. By the end of her painfully long bows, it is clear that "Rose's Turn" was all in her head – but in this case, such a clarification is not needed, for the delusion of the performance has been blatantly obvious since the number's start. Leslie Felperin describes how this sentiment is substantiated by the scene that follows:

> This production keeps in the original happy ending with the final seeming rapprochement between Louise and her mother, but there's a telling sliver of ice in Pulver's delivery that suggests she's only humoring the old lady, whom she'll probably toss away soon like a stripper's glove. (Felperin, 2015)

Comparing Merman, Lansbury, and Staunton in their renditions of "Rose's Turn," it becomes clear that the "authoring" of Rose's madness, while intended by the composers and writers, is truly in the hands of the performers. In a feminist sense, this allows women to reclaim the authorial voice of the madwoman in *Gypsy*. Merman's Rose teeters on the brink of madness, but ultimately brings the audience back to the glamor of Broadway, rather than its realism. Lansbury laid the groundwork for a harsher interpretation of Rose's character. Staunton's rendition of Rose displays the grimmest type of madwoman – but also one who is a gritty, tooth-and-nail fighter; one who is martyred, perhaps, by the circumstances in her life and the confines of her madness.

Conclusion

Gypsy, and especially the character Rose, hold a distinctive and important place in the history of the American musical theater. Rose remains one of the most formidable presences on stage and most prized roles for a performer to play, largely because of her madness. It is a role that displays both singing and acting skills like few others for middle-aged women on Broadway. Rose has become undeniably iconic, so much so that she does not merely represent the stereotype of the crazy backstage mother; she represents the very archetype, invented by *Gypsy*'s creators. When one thinks "show biz momma," one immediately thinks of Momma Rose.

But of course, Rose's quintessence of this character type does not make her one-sided; rather, she is one of the most multifaceted characters in Broadway history, especially compared to other female characters at the time of her origination in 1959. As Clive Barnes states, Rose is "possibly one of the few truly complex characters in the American musical" (Barnes, 1974). Over the decades, critics and scholars have attempted to describe Rose – and performers have tried to embody Rose – in all of her complexity. In these descriptions and enactments of her character, Rose is revealed to be a fascinating, multidimensional figure: a narcissist, a fighter, a dreamer, a sinner, a victim, an anti-hero, and, by the end, a madwoman.

The Rose of *Gypsy: A Musical Fable* expands and recreates the Rose of *Gypsy: A Memoir*, demonstrating the power of music to add dimension to a story and its characters. The music of *Gypsy*, particularly Rose's songs, serves as a powerful source of her character's delineation. As Arthur Laurents argues, *Gypsy* could not have been nearly as successful without its music – and, as shown throughout this document, without music to fashion Rose into a madwoman of operatic proportions. Laurents explains why *Gypsy* could never be a straight play:

> Not the way I wrote it. It's too big. The characters are overblown, the strokes are too bold and too broad … there are fireworks in a scene with about two

> lines and they are screaming and yelling at each other. Music allows you that
> style. The absence of music doesn't . . . the characters tend to be thin unless
> they are filled out by the songs they sing. (Laurents, in Stempel, 2010: 449)

From "Some People" to "Rose's Turn," Rose, through song, tirelessly tackles the fight for her dreams – or, rather, delusions – and constantly, obsessively clashes against a patriarchal system and culture as well as struggling to face her own character flaws.

With the "elevation" of the musical theater genre into the operatic realm with such depth of character, we are left wondering: at what cost? Does Rose's psychological turmoil in "Rose's Turn" elicit sympathy or horror? As Clive Barnes states, Rose is an "activist mother and a born survivor who happened to have been born in slightly the wrong environment. An implacable optimist, she has everything it takes to win, but ends up losing" (Barnes, 1974). Rose's "loss" at the end of her mad scene and of *Gypsy* overall is complicated. She loses her stronghold on her daughter, now grown; she glimpses the reality of her own failed, narcissistic dreams; she grapples with the lack of recognition for her lifelong, tooth-and-nail fight against a culture that Otherizes and overlooks single mothers who refuse to meet sexist norms. Thus, although Rose, like the operatic madwoman trope, does not "win" in the end, her character's conclusion does leave the audience with a hard-earned lesson.

The nuances of Rose's character over the last six decades have been reinterpreted in fascinating ways by many performers, especially in "Rose's Turn." Rose remains iconic, yet the psychological complexity of her character has deepened over the decades. The power of Rose's madness has increased, but the complications that arise therein have also increased, as Rose is performed in front of an ever-evolving audience with improved and nuanced understandings of gender, performance, and general appreciation for psychological difference.

Gypsy's Rose demonstrates an innovative shift away from the ever-present male gaze that permeates most female-centered shows in musical theater history, particularly in the early-mid twentieth-century. *Gypsy*, groundbreakingly, focuses on a female protagonist who not only diverges from the typical ingenue character type but also fails to meet the conventions of romance, sexuality, and domesticity. Authored, in part, by formidable performers on stage and screen, the character of Rose has solidified a remarkable legacy. Examination of her complex character sheds light on the analytical potential for feminist and musicological interpretation of women in musical theater, from the Broadway madwoman's origination with Rose in 1959 to the present day, both in new shows and in new versions of classic productions.

References

Abbate, C. (1991). *Unsung Voices: Opera and Musical Narrative in the Nineteenth Century*. Princeton: Princeton University Press.

Abbate, C. (1993). "Opera or the Envoicing of Women," in Ruth Solie, ed., *Musicology and Difference: Gender and Sexuality in Music Scholarship*. Berkeley: University of California Press, pp. 225–258.

"Angela Lansbury in Gypsy." [Online]. Updated April 22, 2020. www.youtube.com/watch?v=2pA5RWK5qrM. (Accessed September 1, 2024).

"Arthur Laurents in Conversation with David Saint." (2011). Filmmakers Library. [Online]. (Accessed September 20, 2022).

Aston, F. (1959). "'Gypsy,' Ethel Smash Hits," *New York World*, May 22.

(1959). "Merman Has Lungs for Role," *World Telegram*, May 11.

Atkinson, B. (1959). "Merman in 'Gypsy': Topflight Performance in New Musical Play," *The New York Times*, May 31.

Banfield, S. (1993). *Sondheim's Broadway Musicals*. Ann Arbor, MI: University of Michigan Press.

Barnes, C. (1974). "Theater: 'Gypsy' Bounces Back with Zest and Lilt," *The New York Times*, September 24.

Barnes, G. (2015). *Her Turn on Stage: The Role of Women in Musical Theater*. Jefferson, NC: McFarland.

Billington, M. (2015). "Gypsy Review – Imelda Staunton Gives 'One of the Greatest Performances I've Ever Seen in a Musical'," *The Guardian*, April 16.

Cantu, M. (2015). *American Cinderellas on the Broadway Musical Stage: Imagining the Working Girl from Irene to Gypsy*. New York: Palgrave Macmillan.

Chapman, J. (1959). "Miss Merman Has Her Best Role in 'Gypsy,' a Real-Life Musical," *Daily News*, May 22.

Chesler, P. (1972). *Women and Madness*. Chicago, IL: Lawrence Hill Books.

Clapp, S. (2014). "Gypsy Review," *The Observer (London)*, October 19, p. 31.

Clément, C. (1988). *Opera or the Undoing of Women*. Minneapolis, MN: University of Minnesota Press.

Dash, T. R. (1959). "Merman's Performance Proves Tonic to 'Gypsy'," *WWD*, May 22.

Dickson, H. (2022). *Performing Agency – Contemporary Burlesque and the Feminist Gaze*. M. A. Thesis, Toronto: OCAD University.

Dolar, M., and Žižek, S. (2002). *Opera's Second Death*. New York: Routledge.

Engel, L. (2006). *Words with Music: Creating the Broadway Musical Libretto*. Edited by Kissel, H. New York: Applause Theater & Cinema Books.

Everett, W. A., and Laird, P. R. (2016). *Historical Dictionary of the Broadway Musical*. Lanham, MD: Rowman & Littlefield.

Felperin, L. (2015). "'Gypsy': Theater Review," *The Hollywood Reporter*, April 16.

Friedan, B. (1963). *The Feminine Mystique*. New York: W. W. Norton.

Garebian, K. (1994). *The Making of Gypsy*. Toronto: ECW Press.

Gaver, J. (1959). "'Gypsy' Star Talks of New Role: Satisfying to Be Accepted as an 'Actress,' Says Merman," *Morning Telegraph*, June 17.

Gordon, J. (1992). *Art Isn't Easy: The Theater of Stephen Sondheim*. Carbondale, IL: Southern Illinois University Press.

Grant, M. (2004). *The Rise and Fall of the Broadway Musical*. Boston, MA: Northeastern University Press.

Grinenko, A. (2023). *Seriously Mad: Mental Distress and the Broadway Musical*. Ann Arbor, MI: University of Michigan Press.

"The Gypsy Rose Lee Show (1967)." Gypsy Rose Lee Interviews Ethel Merman. [Online]. www.youtube.com/watch?v=gJRQhwzDKWM. (Accessed April 2, 2024).

"Gyspy." (2015). Shout! Factory. [Online]. Amazon Prime Video. (Accessed March 5 2024).

Hulbert, D. (1989). "Reinventing 'Gypsy'," *Chicago Tribune*, October19.

Jenkins, M. B. (2010). *Madness, Sexuality, and Gender in Early Twentieth Century Music Theater Works*: *Four Interpretive Essays*. PhD Dissertation, City University of New York.

Kerr, W. (1959). "First Night Report: Gypsy," *New York Herald Tribune*, May 22.

(1974). "'Gypsy' Is Still Mysteriously Perfect Theater," *The New York Times*, September 29.

Kissel, H. (1993). *David Merrick: The Abominable Showman*. New York: Applause Books.

Knapp, R. (2006). *The American Musical and the Performance of Personal Identity*. Princeton: Princeton University Press.

Ladd-Taylor, M., and Umansky, L. (1998). *"Bad" Mothers: The Politics of Blame in Twentieth-Century America*. New York: New York University Press.

Lahr, J. (2008). "Mother Load: Patti Lupone in 'Gypsy,'" *The New Yorker*, April 7. [Online]. Accessed: February 1, 2021. www.newyorker.com/magazine/2008/04/07/mother-load-2.

Laird, P. R. (2022). *West Side Story, Gypsy, and the Art of Broadway Orchestration*. New York: Routledge.

Laurents, A. (1959). *Gypsy: A Musical* (Original Script).

Laurents, A. (1989). *Gypsy: A Musical*. New York: Theater Communications Group.

Laurents, A. (2000). *Original Story By: A Memoir of Broadway and Hollywood*. New York: Knopf.

Laurents, A. (2009). *Mainly on Directing: Gypsy, West Side Story, and Other Musicals*. New York: Alfred A. Knopf.

Lee, G. R. (1999). *Gypsy: A Memoir*. Berkeley, CA: North Atlantic Books.

Magee, J. (2019). "Whose Turn Is It? Where Gypsy's Finale Came from, and Where It Went," *Studies in Musical Theater* 13 (2), pp. 117–132.

Matsumoto, N. (2004). *The Operatic Mad Scene: Its Origins and Early Development up to c. 1700*. PhD Dissertation. London: Goldsmith's College, University of London.

McClary, S. (1991). *Feminine Endings: Music, Gender, and Sexuality*. [Online]. Minneapolis, MN: University of Minnesota Press. www.amazon.com/ Feminine-Endings-Music-Gender-Sexuality-ebook/dp/B00669KWA2/ ref=tmm_kin_swatch_0?_encoding=UTF8&qid=&sr=. (Accessed: April 10, 2024).

McManus, M. (1959). "The Embodiment of Broadway," *The Baltimore Sun*, October 4.

Miller, D. A. (1998). *Place for Us: Essay on the Broadway Musical*. Cambridge, MA: Harvard University Press.

Mordden, E. (1998). *Coming up Roses: The Broadway Musical in the 1950s*. New York: Oxford University Press.

Mulvey, L. (1975). "Visual Pleasure and Narrative Cinema," *Screen* 16 (3), pp. 6–18.

Oakman, R. (2017). *Momma's Gotta' Let Go: A Character-Driven Analysis of the Mother Archetype in Musical Theater*. M. A. Thesis, York: University of York.

Paulson, M. (2018). "Term of Affection? Ethnic Slur? Theater Union Decides That 'Gypsy' Must Go," *The New York Times*, April 20.

Peikert, M. (2020). "Angela Lansbury Reflects on Her Performance of 'Rose's Turn' in Gypsy." *playbill.com*. [Online], September 23. www.playbill .com/article/angela-lansbury-reflects-on-her-performance-of-roses-turn-in-gypsy. (Accessed December 18, 2023).

Powers, H. S. (1987). "'La Solita Forma' and 'The Uses of Convention,'" *Acta Musicologica* 59 (1), pp. 65–90.

Preminger, E. L. (2012). "Foreword," in Lee G. R., *Mother Finds a Body*. New York: Feminist Press, pp. 5–9.

Quinn, C. (2013). *Mama Rose's Turn: The True Story of America's Most Notorious Stage Mother*. Jackson, MS: University Press of Mississippi.

Rich, F. (2003). "'Gypsy': Then, Now and Always," *The New York Times*, May 4.

Robertson, R. (2014). "'Misfitting' Mothers: Feminism, Disability and Mothering," *Hecate* 40 (1), pp. 7–19.

Schuler, B. (2017). "Let Engeman's 'Gypsy' Entertain You, Yes Sir," *Newsday*, September 10.

Showalter, E. (1985). *The Female Malady: Women, Madness, and English Culture, 1830–1980*. New York: Pantheon Books.

Smart, M. A (1992). "The Silencing of Lucia," *Cambridge Opera Journal* 4 (2) (July), pp. 119–141.

Sondheim, S. (2011). *Finishing the Hat: Collected Lyrics (1954–1981) with Attendant Comments, Principles, Heresies, Grudges, Whines and Anecdotes*. New York: Alfred A. Knopf.

Sondheim, S., and Styne, J. (1959 and 2009). *Gypsy—50th Anniversary Ed. (Original Broadway Cast Recording) Featuring Ethel Merman*. Sony BMG Music Entertainment. [Online] Accessed: May 1, 2020, Spotify.

(1960). *Gypsy (Piano Vocal Score)*. New York: Norbeth Productions.

(1990). *Gypsy (Original London Cast Recording) Featuring Angela Lansbury*. BMG Ariola Argentina S. A. [Online]. Accessed: May 1, 2020, Spotify.

(2008). *Gypsy: The 2008 Broadway Cast Recording Featuring Patti Lupone*. Direct Holdings Americas Inc. [Online]. Accessed: May 1, 2020, Spotify.

(2015). *Gypsy (2015 London Cast Recording) Featuring Imelda Staunton*. Exallshow. [Online]. Accessed May 1, 2020, Spotify.

Stempel, L. (1992). "The Musical Play Expands," *American Music* 10 (2), pp. 136–169.

Stempel, L. (2010). *Showtime: A History of the Broadway Musical Theater*. New York: W. W. Norton.

Steyn, M. (1999). *Broadway Babies Say Goodnight: Musicals Then and Now*. New York: Routledge.

Straus, J. (2018). *Broken Beauty: Musical Modernism and the Representation of Disability*. New York: Oxford University Press.

Styne, J. (2009). "Michael Feinstein Interviews Jule Styne about Composing the Music for 'Gypsy'—Bonus Track." Interview by Michael Feinstein. *Gypsy—50th Anniversary Edition (Original Broadway Cast Recording)*

Featuring Ethel Merman. Sony BMG Music Entertainment. [Online] Accessed: May 1, 2020, Spotify.

Taruskin, R. (2010). *Music in the Nineteenth Century*. New York: Oxford University Press.

Taylor, T. (1979). *Jule: The Story of Composer Jule Styne*. New York: Random House.

Trueman, M. (2015). "West End Review: 'Gypsy' Starring Imelda Staunton." *Variety*, April 16.

Watts Jr., R. (1959). "Ethel Merman Has Another Success." *The New York Post*, May 22.

Wolf, S. (2011). *Changed for Good: A Feminist History of the Broadway Musical*. New York: Oxford University Press.

Wolf, S. (2002). *A Problem Like Maria: Gender and Sexuality in the American Musical*. Ann Arbor, MI: University of Michigan Press.

Worth, J. (2016). "'Who Let in One of Them Mothers?': Maternal Perversity on the American Musical Stage," *Theater History Studies* 35, pp. 255–267.

Zadan, C. (1989). *Sondheim & Co*. New York: Perennial Library.

Musical Theatre

William A. Everett

University of Missouri-Kansas City

William A. Everett, PhD is Curators' Distinguished Professor of Musicology at the University of Missouri-Kansas City Conservatory, where he teaches courses ranging from medieval music to contemporary musical theatre. His publications include monographs on operetta composers Sigmund Romberg and Rudolf Friml and a history of the Kansas City Philharmonic Orchestra. He is contributing co-editor of the *Cambridge Companion to the Musical* and the *Palgrave Handbook of Musical Theatre Producers*. Current research topics include race, ethnicity and the musical and London musical theatre during the 1890s.

About the Series

Elements in Musical Theatre focus on either some sort of "journey" and its resulting dialogue or on theoretical issues. Since many musicals follow a quest model (a character goes in search of something), the idea of a journey aligns closely to a core narrative in musical theatre. Journeys can be, for example, geographic (across bodies of water or land masses), temporal (setting musicals in a different time period than the time of its creation), generic (from one genre to another), or personal (characters in search of some sort of fulfilment). Theoretical issues may include topics relevant to the emerging scholarship on musical theatre from a global perspective and can address social, cultural, analytical and aesthetic perspectives.